100 ATHLETES

WHO SHAPED SPORTS HISTORY

TIMOTHY JACOBS
RUSSELL ROBERTS

sourcebooks
eXplore

Copyright © 2003, 2023 by Sourcebooks
Text by Timothy Jacobs and Russell Roberts
Cover design by Will Riley
Internal illustrations by Westchester Publishing Services
Cover and internal design © 2023 by Sourcebooks

Published by Sourcebooks eXplore, an imprint of Sourcebooks Kids
P.O. Box 4410, Naperville, Illinois 60567–4410
(630) 961-3900
sourcebookskids.com

Originally published in 2003 by Bluewood Books, a division of The Siyeh Group, Inc.

Cataloging-in-Publication Data is on file with the Library of Congress.

Source of Production: Versa Press, East Peoria, Illinois, USA
Date of Production: July 2023
Run Number: 5032107

Printed and bound in the United States of America.
VP 10 9 8 7 6 5 4 3 2 1

CONTENTS

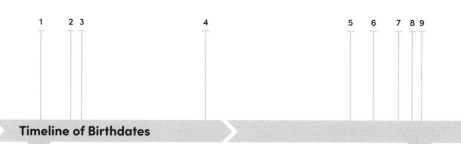

1   2 3   4   5   6   7 8 9

Timeline of Birthdates

600 BCE   1875

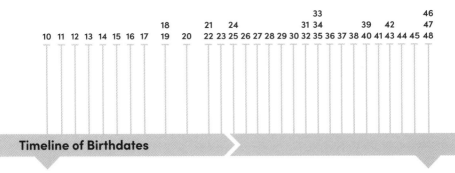

Timeline of Birthdates

1876

1940

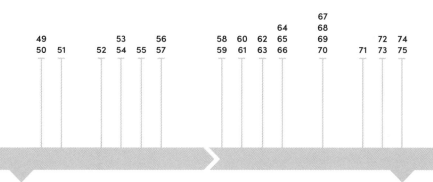

1941   1960

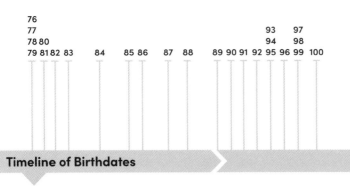

Timeline of Birthdates

1961

2000

INTRODUCTION

SPORTS ARE an integral part of the human experience. Athletic competition serves as a barometer of society's progress as well as a measure of human sacrifice, dedication, and aspiration.

This book describes the achievements of one hundred extraordinary people from all over the world across the entire spectrum of sports. Beginning with the legendary wrestlers and runners of ancient Greece and Rome and continuing on to baseball and football superstars of the twenty-first century and more, these one hundred biographies highlight the accomplishments of some of the most skilled and talented athletes in sports history.

In the past, organized sporting activity mainly flourished when civilizations surpassed basic survival mode—the stage when economic and cultural development allows resources to be diverted into the development and training of athletes. Nations are proud of their sports heroes; they represent the vigor and vitality of their country. Whether it is an Olympian winning a gold medal or a professional baseball player smashing home runs in a World Series game, sports fans revel in these accomplishments as a reflection of their country.

Beyond that, however, we follow sports so closely because we see ourselves in the athletes. In the image of **Michael Jordan** sinking a last-minute jumper or **Megan Rapinoe** sending the perfect corner kick straight for a game-winning goal, we see ourselves. Every kid who throws a football, does a somersault in the gym, or finishes a lap in the pool imagines themselves perhaps as a future **Joe Montana**, **Nadia Comăneci**, or **Michael Phelps**.

As for the athletes themselves, men and women such as **Jim Thorpe**, **Pat McCormick**, **Johnny Unitas**, **Martina Navratilova**, and **Bethany Hamilton** have proven that the desire to excel—even despite great odds—can be a driving force within the human spirit. Many athletes sacrificed greatly, trained rigorously, and in some cases overcame great obstacles to reach the peak of athletic perfection. Perhaps that is why it is so hard for some to admit when age and injuries have taken a toll on their once awesome skills and acknowledge that it is time retire. It is difficult to admit that something to which you've relentlessly dedicated many years of your life is over—often at an age when most other people are just reaching their prime.

This book describes the prime athletic years of these individuals—the times when remarkable men and women accomplished feats that may have even amazed themselves while they thrilled hundreds or thousands of sports fans. It is about those people who oftentimes proved so adept or so skillful that they not only broke records but changed the very way a game is played or perceived. It is about, many times, perfection—and that is a rare quality to find anywhere else in life.

With that said, enjoy the stories of these one hundred athletes. Admire their dedication and delight in their achievements because, in the final analysis, they are in many ways our heroes.

◆ Born in Croton (a colony of the ancient Achaean Greeks, now Crotone, Calabria in Italy) in 558 BCE, **MILO** was as large in life as most Greek heroes were in myth. His athletic career, which coincided with the era of the original Olympic Games, spanned twenty-five years and brought him much notoriety. He may have been the most dominant athlete in any sport of all time. As an ancient writer put it: "Neither God nor man could stand against him!"

Legend says that Milo developed his great strength by carrying a calf every day from its birth until it was a full-grown ox. It is also said that he carried an ox across the entire length of the stadium at Olympia. The weight of the animal is estimated to have been at least 900 pounds, and the length of the stadium over 600 feet (approximately 630 feet today).

Milo was the wrestling champion in 32 games on record: six Olympian, seven Pythian, nine Nemean, and ten Isthmian Games. These were the four most important sports festivals (known as *agons* in Greek), gathering athletes from Olympia, Delphi, Nemea, and the Isthmus of Corinth to all compete together in a cycle of tournaments known collectively as the Panhellenic Games. Each of these tournaments was held quadrennially—every four years—just as the Olympics are today. In the rare event that an athlete won all four tournaments in one circuit (or *períodos*), they were hailed as *periodoníkēs*, the equivalent of a grand-slam winner today. Milo won this honorary title five times in recorded history. According to two different accounts, he failed to win his seventh Olympics only because either wrestling was canceled when none of his competitors had the courage to show up, or because his lone competitor, an athlete named **Timastheos**, refused to come near him after her entered the wrestling arena.

Milo was one the greatest of all ancient Olympian athletes. As was sometimes the practice with highly revered athletes, a huge bronze statue was created in his honor. The statue, however, had to be transported to the Altis (meaning "high place") at Olympia, and no one could engineer a way to do it. Rather than be dishonored, Milo picked the statue up and carried it to the Altis himself.

The traditional account of Milo's death is that he found a tree that some woodcutters had partially split open with a wedge. When he tried to finish the job and tear the tree apart, the wedge fell out, and the tree closed on his hand. Trapped, he could not defend himself from wild wolves who were then able to devour him.

PHIDIPPIDES was an Athenian Greek. He was a trained athletic runner and messenger who set a rare example of dedication, courage, and stamina. He also unwittingly established what is now known as a **marathon** by running twenty-six miles nonstop from the Greek city of Marathon to Athens, to bring news of the Greek victory over the Persians in the Battle of Marathon.

As a runner, Phidippides made his mark in the ancient world just shortly before making his historic run. In 490 BCE, the Persian army had landed a large force on the Marathon plains just outside of Athens and prepared to attack the Greek city. Greatly outnumbered, the Athenians decided to ask the city of Sparta for help in fighting off their enemy. The Athenian generals sent Phidippides, a professional runner, to Sparta to deliver the plea for support.

The distance between the two cities was approximately 140 miles over very mountainous and rugged terrain, but Phidippides covered it in about thirty-six hours. After delivering the message, Phidippides ran back to Athens with the response—Sparta agreed to help but only when the moon was full—meaning that he ran about 280 miles in seventy-two hours! It should also be noted that he did this either barefoot or wearing sandals.

Knowing that they couldn't wait that long for the Spartan reinforcements, the Athenian army—including Phidippides in full battle armor—marched out to face the Persians. They unleashed a surprise offensive that caught the Persians off guard and defeated them. The remaining Persians set sail south for the city of Athens to try and capture it before the Athenian army could return.

The Athenian army then sent Phidippides racing to Athens to carry news of their great victory over the Persians and to warn of their approaching ships. Despite his previous efforts—running 280 miles and then fighting in full armor—Phidippides ran the twenty-six miles to Athens in about three hours. Reaching the city, he is said to have cried, "Be happy! We have won!" He then died of exhaustion.

The stamina and courage of Phidippides are evoked whenever a runner of extraordinary marathon ability becomes well-known.

Phidippides set an inspired example for all runners to follow. That he established one of the great racing distances—and that it remains in use even today—is an "endurance record" of another kind of almost twenty-five hundred years!

In the ancient world, the pentathlon was a competitive sporting event comprising the long jump, discus throw, wrestling, 200-yard dash, and javelin throw. The most famous of all Greek athletes at this event was **PHAYLLOS OF CROTON**.

Phayllos won the pentathlon at the Pythian Games at Delphi twice and was also a champion runner in events apart from the pentathlon. He performed his athletic feats within a century after **Milo of Croton** had amazed the ancient world with his legendary athletic ability.

One of Phayllos's greatest accomplishments was making a 55-foot-long jump. This is one the few exact measurements of an athletic achievement recorded in antiquity. Even though this was in Delphic feet, which were approximately seven inches long, it still makes his jump equal to thirty-two feet today. What also must be taken into account is that Greek long jumpers used four-pound weights in each hand to add momentum to their jumps, although the take-off run was comparatively short and may have offset the advantage of using weights.

Another of Phayllos's legendary feats in competition was a 95-foot discus throw. However, this is almost impossible to compare with current discus records, since the discus in Phayllos's day was made of stone, ranged in weight from 2.75 pounds to 12.5 pounds, and came in various sizes. We have to assume that ancient people took these variances into account when establishing championships. The Greek style of discus throwing also involved moving only one step forward, and the discus was thrown in a vertical arc approximately seven inches long.

However, we have the authority of such eminent ancient writers as **Herodotus, Pausanias, Zenobius,** and **Scholion**—who all wrote much after Phayllos's time—to say that he was one of the greatest ancient athletes.

◆ Of all the Roman emperors who took up the bow and arrow as a sport seriously, Roman Emperor **DOMITIAN** was probably one of the most important in establishing archery as a pastime.

His skill level was reportedly very high. For exhibitions, he would have a servant stand several yards away from him. The servant then held his hand out away from his body and stretched his fingers wide. Domitian would shoot an arrow between each of the servant's fingers, without so much as grazing him.

Legend says that the emperor killed up to one hundred wild animals in a single day at Alba. According to the story, he drew his bow with such skill and quickness that he could shoot two arrows in rapid succession into the head of the animal.

Domitian's proficiency with the bow and arrow inspired others to take up archery, firmly establishing it as a sport in ancient Rome. In fact, one of the emperors who succeeded him, **Commodus** (161–192 CE), put on archery exhibitions in the Roman arena.

This was an important milestone in the development of archery, since Romans tended to view bows and arrows as weapons of their enemies—Greeks and Persians, for example—and not their own.

Domitian also established Greek Olympic-style games in Rome. While Greek games took place in Roman-held Greek colonies after Rome became the dominant power in the Mediterranean, Domitian established the first regular Greek-style athletic contests on Roman soil.

Domitian named these games the Capitoline Games. They were immediately included in the list of Greek Sacred Games and were seen as second only to the Olympics themselves.

The Capitoline Games were quadrennial and had three main contest divisions. These were music, equestrian, and gymnastics, and even included races for the maidens (women were generally forbidden from participating in the ancient Greek games). There was also singing, accompaniment, and solo instrumental performances.

While historians may judge Domitian's political rule as emperor, it is clear he did make positive advancements in several realms of the sports world.

5 THOMAS TOPHAM

1710-1749

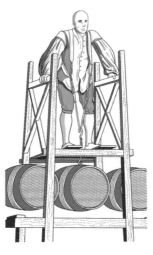

◆ Student of physical culture **David Willoughby** theorizes in his book, *The Super Athletes*, that some individuals are true prodigies, being naturally endowed to outperform the rest of us. Willoughby's conception of physical prodigies is that they are simply built differently than the rest of us—tendons are attached to bone in a way that leads to superior muscular leverage, their glands secrete just a little more strength-giving substance than the average person—and that accounts for strength that is disproportionate to height and weight.

THOMAS TOPHAM, an eighteenth-century British innkeeper, was a physical prodigy who demonstrated amazing strength during his short but extraordinary life.

Topham was not an overly large man; he stood five-feet, ten-inches tall and weighed 196 pounds. Yet, he was the strong man upon whom all the strong men after him have based their routines.

Topham was the son of a carpenter, and although he trained for his father's profession, he became manager of London's Red Lion Inn at the age of twenty-five. This was right around the time that he suffered a lifelong injury—he was restraining two draft horses in an exhibition when the ground gave way, and he shattered a kneecap. Remarkably, even though this serious injury was at the start of his amazing career, it did not prevent him from achieving incredible feats.

Reportedly, Topham could bend an inch-thick iron poker around a man's neck like a bow tie, and then "untie" it easily. This was a feat that he supposedly demonstrated once when a customer insulted him, and Topham decided to embarrass the man.

Topham's hand strength was such that he once crushed a coconut in one hand the way that a cook cracks an egg. He could also snap pipe stems in his outstretched fingers and could crush pipe bowls by squashing them with his thumb and index finger. He carried a full-grown horse over a gate and lifted 224 pounds over his head with just his pinky. He is also said to have once lifted a 378-pound man using only one arm.

However, those feats pale before his most notable public exhibition, when he performed a harness lift of three heavy casks weighing 1,836 pounds in total while standing on a platform. He did this at a large celebration in honor of the British victory at the Spanish port of Cartagena on April 1, 1741.

If that was all that Topham was credited with, he would have carved out an impressive niche in the world of weightlifting. But there was more. He supposedly carried a sleeping sentry and his sentry box several blocks to confuse the man when he woke up. He also seized hold of the rear end of a horse-drawn carriage and pulled it backward, even as the carriage's team of horses struggled to go forward. He even managed to jog for a half-mile while carrying a 336-pound barrel of nails.

Unfortunately, great physical strength does not guarantee protection against life's various trials, as Topham learned. One day, he stormed out of his home after quarreling with his wife and injured himself. He died as a result of that injury on August 10, 1749.

SULTAN SELIM III was a Turkish ruler whose archery skills were so great that he set a record in the sport that went uncontested for almost two centuries.

Traditionally, archery was seen as the sport of emperors and kings. Roman Emperor **Domitian** (see no. 4), for one, was a noted archer in the first century. During the Ottoman Empire, the Turkish court also took this tradition very seriously. The Turkish bow was more than just a weapon as it was associated with sacred and symbolic functions. The sons of Ottoman sultans learned bow-and-arrow skills that they often continued to practice when they became rulers.

Selim III's skill was as a bow maker. Thus, he was a natural candidate to settle a simmering dispute between the English and Turks about archery in 1798.

Two years prior, a Turkish ambassador visiting England had boasted loudly that Turkish bows were better than English bows. The English, who trace their archery ancestry back to ancient times, proposed that the ambassador prove his boast.

The Turkish ambassador agreed; he selected an old bow from the era of the Seljuk Turks (1000–1300) and shot an arrow from it. The arrow traveled 482 yards, which at the time would have been a long-distance record with a modern bow.

This incident was still on everyone's mind in 1798 when Sultan Selim III decided to set the matter straight once and for all in front of the British ambassador, Sir **Robert Ainslie**.

The sultan unsheathed an arrow and placed it on his bow, which was quite probably one he had made himself, given his background. He then most likely set himself in the "freestyle" position—in which the archer lies on his back, braces his feet against the bow,

and pulls the string back with both hands—and let the arrow fly.

The arrow soared an incredible 972 yards and 2.75 inches. Ainslie himself confirmed the distance as a world record that lasted almost two hundred years. Unfortunately for the sultan, his record made out better than he did. He was deposed in 1807 and executed in 1808.

KANŌ JIGORŌ was the founder of judo, the first Japanese martial arts to gain worldwide popularity as it was the first to become an Olympic sport. Kanō was an athlete, but he was also an educator. In his youth, he began practicing jujitsu to strengthen his body. Jujitsu is a martial art that uses throwing, holding, choking, hitting, and kicking to block an opponent. Over time, he started to change and adapt the practice into something that better fit his needs and that he felt better matched what modern people needed. Judo's aim is to build character. If you have heard of judo, it is thanks to Kanō.

Kanō Jigorō was born in 1860 in Mikage, Japan. His interest in more combative forms of classic jujitsu led him to change the sport in such positive ways that he soon went on to become an educator and director of primary education for the Ministry of Education from 1898 to 1901. After that, he was president of Tokyo Higher Normal School from 1901–1920. He was the reason that physical exercise and judo became a part of Japanese public education.

Kanō founded and served as director of the Kodokan Judo Hall in 1882, and he made efforts to study and popularize judo throughout his entire life. Kanō's impact on international sports was powerful, and he was the first Asian member of the International Olympic Committee. Today, the International Judo Federation (IJF) includes representatives from 195 countries and regions.

Innovations in teaching style attributed to Kanō include the use of black and white belts to show the ranking between members of a martial art style. Well-known mottos attributed to Kanō include "Maximum efficiency with minimum effort" and "Mutual welfare and benefit."

Judo is taught under two methods: Randori and Kata. Randori, or "free exercise," is practiced under conditions of actual contest. It includes throwing, choking, holding down, and bending or twisting the opponent's arms or legs. The combatants may use whatever tricks they like, provided they do not hurt each other and obey the general rules of judo etiquette. Kata, which literally means "form," is a formal system of prearranged exercises, including hitting and kicking and the use of weapons. According to the rules, each person knows beforehand exactly what his opponent is going to do. The use of weapons and hitting and kicking is taught in Kata but not in Randori.

Among other honors, Kanō was awarded the First Order of Merit, recognition by the Order of the Rising Sun. He was inducted into the IJF Hall of Fame in 1999 and passed away on May 4, 1938, at the age of seventy-seven.

HARRY VARDON is one of the most revered figures in golf history. In addition to winning six British Open championships from 1896 to 1914, he was the runner-up in that tournament four times.

Unlike many other great golfers, Vardon did not grow up in a golfing environment. Born William Henry Vardon, he worked as a gardener for a man who enjoyed golf and who sometimes let him caddie.

Vardon's employer would also let him use his equipment to play a few strokes. Curious as to his level of skill, Vardon entered a few tournaments. When he won one and finished second in the other, he turned professional.

In 1896, at Muirfield in East Lothian, Scotland, Vardon defeated **J. H. Taylor** 157 to 161 in thirty-six holes to win his first British Open. He was the first Englishman to win the tournament.

In 1900, Vardon visited the United States. That year, at the United States Golf Association (USGA) Open at the Chicago Golf Club in Wheaton, Illinois, he beat Taylor again to win that tournament. Vardon went on to tour the country, won all but one of eighty-eight exhibitions he played, and helped popularize the growth of golf in America.

In 1913, Vardon made a second visit to the United States and entered that year's USGA U.S. Open, which was held at the Country Club in Brookline, Massachusetts. In one of golf's greatest matches, Vardon was tied at the end of regulation play with Englishman **Ted Ray** and an up-and-coming twenty-year-old American named **Francis Ouimet**. The next day, Vardon finished runner-up to Ouimet, who won the eighteen-round playoff.

Vardon was golf's first international celebrity and is credited with devising the first modern golf swing. He was also said to be a cantankerous man who did not mince words. A story has it that he was playing a round of golf with eighteen-year-old **Bobby Jones** (see no. 17) in Toledo, Ohio. Though later a man of grace and reserved self-control, Jones had a perfectionist's bad temper when he was young.

Vardon and Jones were fairly even when the brash young Jones knocked his ball into a bunker. In disgust, Jones turned to Vardon and said, "Did you ever see a worse shot?" Vardon then spoke for the first and last time that day: "No." From that day forward, Jones learned to control his emotions.

In 1920, at the age of fifty and following two bouts of tuberculosis, Vardon tied for second place in the U.S. Open. In addition to his outstanding play over the years, Vardon also did course alterations, such as at the great Irish Royal County Down course in Newcastle.

RAY EWRY was truly an amazing athlete. He overcame a childhood disease that left him confined to a wheelchair to become a champion athlete and winner of ten Olympic gold medals.

Ewry was born in 1873, in Lafayette, Indiana. He contracted polio when he was young, and he was told by his doctor that he would never be able to walk or move around independently. Despite this dire prognosis, Ewry set up his own exercise regimen. He gradually built up strength in his legs and became so athletic that he could play football and compete in track-and-field at Purdue University.

After he graduated from Purdue, Ewry moved to New York City, where he joined the New York Athletic Club (NYAC) and competed in track-and-field.

Ewry was one of several NYAC athletes to compete in the 1900 Olympics in Paris, France. On July 16, 1900, he won gold medals in three events: standing high jump, standing long jump, and standing triple jump. Four years later, he won gold medals in the same three events at the Olympics held in the United States, in St. Louis, Missouri.

The standing triple jump was eliminated from the Olympics after 1904, but Ewry kept competing. He won gold medals in the standing high jump and standing long jump in 1906. Because those victories occurred outside the regular four-year Olympic Games cycle, they were not regarded as part of the official record.

However, it mattered little to Ewry. He again won gold in the standing high jump and standing long jump in the 1908 Olympics. He tried again for the Olympics in 1912, but he did not make the team.

The standing jumps were regular Amateur Athletic Union (AAU) events in Ewry's time. Often, standing jump athletes held weights in their hands to add momentum. The following are some of Ewry's best performances without weights: a standing high jump of 5 feet in Paris in 1906; a mark of 34 feet, 8 1/2 inches in the standing hop, step, and jump in Paris in 1906; and he jumped 11 feet, 6 inches in the standing broad jump in New York City in 1906.

After failing to make the Olympic team in 1912, Ewry retired from athletics and became an engineer. He died in 1937. In 1974, he was inducted into the National Track and Field Hall of Fame, and in 1983 was made a member of the U.S. Olympic Hall of Fame.

A superb figure skater who won a record-holding ten men's world championships, **ULRICH SALCHOW** also invented a skating maneuver that is still prominently used by skaters today: the **salchow jump**.

Born Karl Emil Julius Ulrich Salchow in 1877 in Stockholm, Sweden, Salchow won the first of his World Figure Skating Championships in 1901, and then reeled off a string of four more from 1902 to 1905.

Salchow's streak was broken in 1906, but he came back to win five more consecutive world championships from 1907 to 1911. He also won the European Championships nine times, another record, between 1898 and 1913. He was the first athlete to win an Olympic gold medal for skating in 1908, and is still one of the oldest figure skating Olympic champions at age 31.

The skating maneuver Salchow invented is one of the most difficult in the sport. In the salchow jump, the skater takes off from the rear inside edge of one skate, completes one, two, or three revolutions, and lands on the rear outside edge of the skate. The jump is varied by the number of revolutions the skater makes, for example, a triple salchow would involve three revolutions. Salchow first landed this move in 1909, and it later became known as the Salchow jump in honor.

Salchow was president of the International Skating Union from 1925 to 1937, and was also involved in other sports, serving on the Swedish Amateur Boxing Committee from 1919 to 1932.

Salchow is remembered not only as a multiple record-breaking athlete, but also as a very generous person who respected and publicly acknowledged the talents of his competitors. He died at age 71 in Stockholm on April 19, 1949.

He was the great-grandson of American railway and shipping baron **Cornelius Vanderbilt**, but more significantly for the sports world, **HAROLD VANDERBILT** was a superb yachtsman.

Harold Vanderbilt was born in 1884 into a world of nearly unprecedented luxury thanks to his family's wealth. As a young man, he decided to focus his energy on yacht racing instead of the family business of running the New York Central Railroad. Yacht racing in the nineteenth and early twentieth centuries featured professional pilots, but Vanderbilt changed that. He was an amateur who won the America's Cup—the World Series of yacht racing—three times for the New York Yacht Club. Since Vanderbilt's time, amateur pilots have continued to dominate the sport.

It was fitting that this new kind of pilot would command a new type of racing yacht, built in tune with a new classification. The boats that Vanderbilt piloted to victory were called "J" boats, named for their sequence in the classifications. The J-boats had 75–87-foot-long waterlines and featured single, massive triangular mainsails with overlapping jibs. Later on, they also boasted parachute spinnakers.

Vanderbilt proposed further innovations on the 80-foot-long boat called *The Enterprise,* the J-boat he would pilot to his first America's Cup victory in 1930. These innovations included a unique "Park Avenue boom," with runners and slides that would allow aerodynamic shaping of the mainsail coupled with a 162-foot-high mainmast made of two hollow tubes of lightweight duralumin—half the weight of a conventional mast. Other innovations included a unique double centerboard to help with sailing into the wind and running before the wind as well as more than two dozen winches to handle the ship's lines.

The Enterprise beat Irish tea merchant **Sir Thomas Lipton's** boat *Shamrock V* in the 1930 America's Cup races; the cup went to the winner of the best four out of seven. However, when international opinion rose up against *The Enterprise*, Vanderbilt built a new boat called the *Rainbow*. This yacht beat Englishman Thomas Sopwith's boat *Endeavour* four races to two.

The greatest J-boat, though, was Vanderbilt's *Ranger*, which due to the Great Depression, was built at cost by a shipyard and fitted with rigging from Vanderbilt's two previous J-boats. This yacht beat Sopwith's *Endeavour II* in four straight races in 1937.

The deepening Depression, developing tensions leading up to World War II, and the after-tax structure spelled the end for extravagant J-boats. Yachting, however, was not Harold Vanderbilt's only passion; he is also credited with inventing the game of **contract bridge**.

At the 1912 Olympic Games, the King of Sweden said to **JIM THORPE** what everyone else in the world was thinking: "Sir, you are the greatest athlete in the world."

Today, more than a half-century after his death, many people consider James Francis Thorpe the best all-around athlete of all time.

Thorpe was born near present-day Prague, Oklahoma, which at the time, was American Indian territory. His ancestry was part **Sac and Fox Indian**, as well as Irish and Welsh. His original American Indian name was **Wa-thohuck** (meaning "Bright Path").

In 1907, Thorpe attended the Carlisle Indian School in Pennsylvania. He made a name for himself in football and track but left the school in 1909 for North Carolina. There, he played semipro baseball.

In 1911, he returned to Carlisle. His play on the varsity football team was the major reason that Carlisle beat some of the best college teams of the era. He made the all-American team in 1911 and 1912.

Thorpe also excelled in other sports during this period. He could high jump 6 feet, 5 inches, pole vault 11 feet, run the 100-yard dash in 10 seconds flat and the 220-yard dash in 21.8 seconds. What's more, he threw the discus 136 feet, the javelin 163 feet, and the hammer 140 feet, and he ran the mile in 4 minutes and 35 seconds.

In 1912, Thorpe went to the Olympic Games in Stockholm, Sweden, as a member of the U.S. team. He won gold medals in both the pentathlon and the decathlon. However, in 1913 the AAU learned of his time playing semipro baseball in North Carolina, and they stripped him of his medals.

Thorpe joined major league baseball's New York Giants in 1913. A weak hitter, he never excelled at the game and retired in 1919. However, Thorpe's real love was football, and he was a true star. In 1915, he had organized the Canton Bulldogs professional football team and played on that team for a then-lordly $500 per game. He was an excellent runner, a fine passer, and a terrific kicker.

In 1920, the American Professional Football Association was established, with Thorpe as the first president; it later became the National Football League in 1922. Thorpe played with the Bulldogs until he retired in 1929. He subsequently acted in movies, lectured on American Indian culture, and served in the U.S. Merchant Marine.

In 1950, Thorpe was selected as the greatest all-around athlete and football player of the first half of the twentieth century by nearly 400 American broadcasters and sportswriters. In 1983, the International Olympic Committee posthumously restored his Olympic medals.

TAZIO NUVOLARI'S skill behind the wheel was legendary. Known as *Il montavani volante*—the **"Flying Mantuan"**—he won thirty of the most important races held in Europe between 1921 and 1939.

Nuvolari was born in 1892, in Casteldrio, near Mantua, Italy, and got his start racing motorcycles at age twenty-eight. At the Monza Grand Prix for motorcycles, he broke both his legs during practice. Despite being told that it would be a month before he could walk again, Nuvolari raced the next day by tying himself to the bike. He won the race.

In 1924, at the age of thirty-two, Nuvolari began racing automobiles. In the 1930 Mille Miglia (Thousand Miles), he caught the unsuspecting leader while driving at night without his headlights. Three kilometers from the finish line, Nuvolari suddenly pulled alongside his rival, smiled at him, flicked on his headlights, and roared to victory.

Perhaps Nuvolari's greatest win came in the 1935 Grand Prix of Germany. Driving an aging red Alfa Romeo, he was up against the fastest race cars in the world: the 180-mph Auto-Union cars and the 175-mph Mercedes-Benz machines driven by some of the best drivers in Europe. His Alfa was 20 mph slower.

It was a mountainous course with 175 curves, measuring fourteen miles per lap. By the tenth lap, Nuvolari had risen from sixth to first place. Then his crew bungled a refueling stop, dropping him back to sixth place. By the thirteenth lap, Nuvolari had regained second and was pushing the first-place car so hard that it ran its tires ragged and had a blowout halfway through the last lap. Nuvolari roared on by to win by thirty-two seconds.

Throughout his career, Nuvolari drove in 172 races. He won sixty-four of them and placed second sixteen times and third nine times against the toughest competition of his era. Nuvolari had a tremendous desire to win—even at the cost of jeopardizing his health. In 1947, he drove for Ferrari and won twice, despite being hypersensitive to racing fuel because of tuberculosis. His lungs hemorrhaged.

Despite his illness, Nuvolari almost won the Mille Miglia a third time. Unfortunately, some water in his magneto slowed his car within sight of the finish line, allowing the second-place driver to pass him. In 1947, he was thirty minutes ahead of the competition in the Mille when his Ferrari broke down. Two years later, he won at Monte Pellegrino, but had to be lifted out of his car, spitting blood.

On August 11, 1953, nine months after suffering a stroke, Nuvolari died. He was buried in his uniform—a yellow jersey and blue trousers.

◆ Martial artist **IP MAN** not only made a name for himself as an expert in **Wing Chun** but also became known as a respected teacher who trained future martial arts masters.

Ip Man was born on October 1, 1893, into a wealthy family in Foshan, in the Guangdong province of China. He began studying martial arts when he was a young boy. This included Wing Chun, a Chinese martial art and form of self-defense that uses quick kicks and arm movements against opponents. Ip's first teacher, **Chan Wah-shun,** was a grandmaster in Wing Chun.

When Ip was sixteen, he moved to Hong Kong to complete secondary school at St. Stephen's College. Through a classmate, Ip met Leung Bik, the son of a respected Wing Chun practitioner. Confident in his own abilities, Ip challenged Leung to a sparring match, and Leung agreed, quickly beating Ip twice. Despite Ip's losses, Leung was impressed with Ip's talent, and Ip began training under Leung.

Ip returned to his hometown of Foshan and became a police officer there when he was twenty-four, all the while teaching Wing Chun casually to friends and colleagues. He married Cheung Wing-sing, and after the two started a family, Ip began teaching his children the martial art too.

In 1949, the Chinese Communist Party won the Chinese Civil War. Because Ip was a member of the opposition party, he feared for his safety. Ip, Cheung, and their daughter fled to Hong Kong in 1950. Cheung soon returned to Foshan to retrieve some items they had left behind, but in 1951 borders between Hong Kong and China were closed, permanently separating Ip and his wife.

Ip started a martial arts school in Hong Kong, offering young martial artists formal training in Wing Chun. He trained many students, including **Bruce Lee**, an actor and martial artist who went on to star in many blockbuster movies and TV shows that featured martial arts.

Though Ip died of cancer in 1972, his legacy was carried on by his students. Many followed Ip's example and opened their own schools, spreading the practice of Wing Chung wider, and bringing worldwide attention to Ip's name by crediting him as their trainer.

JACK DEMPSEY was a gentle man outside the boxing ring, but when he donned his gloves, he became the "**Manassa Mauler**," doing a rhythmic, shuffling dance and humming an almost inaudible tune, whose beat was the cadence of his punches.

He was born **William Harrison Dempsey** in the mining town of Manassa, Colorado, in 1895. Although he worked full shifts in the mines as a teenager, his real goal was to be a prizefighter. Setting out on his own, he fought in the back room of saloons. In 1917, he linked up with manager **Jack "Doc" Kearns**, who arranged fights with top-ranked heavyweights for Dempsey.

Dempsey won twenty-one fights in 1918—seventeen by knockout. The following year, the 187-pound Dempsey fought 245-pound **Jess Willard** for the championship. He knocked Willard down seven times in the first round. By the third round, Willard conceded defeat. Later, Dempsey's manager, who was bitter after legal battles with the fighter, claimed that he had loaded Dempsey's gloves with plaster of paris. However, sports-writers later tested that claim and found that the plaster would, if anything, have softened Dempsey's blows.

In 1921, the crafty Kearns used a charge that Dempsey had been a World War I draft dodger to stage the first million-dollar prize-fight in history between Dempsey and war hero **Georges Carpentier**. Carpentier lost in four rounds, and the draft-dodging charge was later disproved in court.

In 1923, one of the most ferocious heavy-weight bouts of the twentieth century took place, between Dempsey and **Luis Firpo**, known as the "Bull of the Pampas." In the first round alone, Firpo dropped Dempsey seconds into the fight, then Dempsey knocked Firpo down six times, and finally, Firpo knocked Dempsey completely out of

the ring. In the second round, the champ knocked Firpo out.

In 1926, after three years of inactivity, Dempsey lost his title in a decision to **Gene Tunney**, who out-boxed him. In the return match the following year, Dempsey knocked Tunney down for what has become known as "the long count." Tunney stayed down on the floor for fourteen seconds, but because Dempsey failed to retreat to a neutral cor-ner, the referee delayed the count. This gave Tunney time to recover, and he later won the bout.

After the second fight with Tunney, Dempsey retired. He won sixty pro bouts during his career, with forty-nine by knock-out and only seven loses. In 1950, he was voted the Best Boxer of the Half-Century by an Associated Press poll.

Dempsey went on to represent the box-ing world as a public figure and to referee some fights. He also ran a well-known and popular restaurant in New York City for many years.

PAAVO NURMI, nicknamed the **"Flying Finn,"** was an exceptional long-distance runner. He set twenty-three world records from 1921–1931, in events ranging from the 1,500-meter race to the 20,000-meter race.

Nurmi was born to a poor family in Abo, Finland, in 1897. Although he had to work at an early age, he still found time to run and to display exceptional promise. In World War I, Nurmi became a soldier, yet he continued to train as a runner. He was a common sight in the early morning, running for several miles along the icy roads and returning in time for reveille.

Once the war ended, Nurmi began systematic note-taking, comparing his time with the times of other runners, and calculating exactly at which points in a race to simply stride versus when to run his fastest. He often carried a stopwatch in practice and in the more important races, which he would use to time his progress. Interestingly, he threw the watch away as he began the final lap.

Before Nurmi began using these methods, most runners would usually jog until the last two laps, and then pour all they had into the finish. However, Nurmi's use of a stopwatch enabled him to maintain a steady pace and run at a consistent speed. His methods had a great influence on the development of the sport of competitive running.

At the 1920 Olympics, Nurmi won gold medals in the 10,000-meter race and the 10,000-meter cross-country race. In addition, he led the Finnish squad to victory in the team category of the latter event.

In June 1921, Nurmi set world records for the 10,000-meter with a time of 30:40.2 and the 6-mile run, clocking in at 28:41.2. Over the next two years, he added three more records: a time of 14:35.2 for the 5,000 meters, 3:52.6 for the 1,500 meters, and 4:10.4 for the mile.

At the 1924 Olympic Games, Finnish officials prevented Nurmi from competing in the 10,000-meter race to allow other Finnish runners a chance to place. Nevertheless, Nurmi won five gold medals at those Olympics, including the 1,500- and 5,000-meter races. Amazingly, he won these races despite the fact that the events were only fifty-five minutes apart!

Nurmi won a gold medal in the 10,000-meter race in the 1928 Olympics and went on to set records in distance running up until July 1931, when he ran two miles in a record 8:59.5. He was not allowed to compete in the 1932 Olympics because it was ruled that he had lost his amateur status when it came to light that he had accepted money for training. His last victory in a race came in 1933 at the Finnish National Championship.

Considered by many to be the greatest golfer in history, **BOBBY JONES** is the only player to win the sport's fabled Grand Slam. (At the time, the Grand Slam meant a golfer had to win the U.S. Open, the British Open, the U.S. Amateur, and the British Amateur championships in the same year.) When he retired from the game, he founded one of golf 's most prestigious tournaments.

He was born Robert Tyre Jones Jr., in 1902 in Atlanta, Georgia. He took up golf only when his parents moved near the Atlanta Country Club (ACC). Jones mastered the game quickly; when he was nine, he became AAC'S junior champion. At age fourteen, he entered his first U.S. Amateur tournament. Young Jones had a fiery temper that hurt his game, but help from his colleagues enabled him to control it. Thereafter, he was the epitome of a perfect gentleman out on the green.

Jones won the first of four U.S. Open titles in 1923, but he still felt that he was struggling as a golfer. That was when he decided that he was worrying too much about the competition. Soon, he became determined to only worry about achieving par and launched himself on a string of remarkable victories.

Jones won the U.S. Open in 1926, 1929, and 1930. He was U.S. Amateur champion five times in 1924, 1925, 1927, 1928, and 1930, and he won the British Open in 1926, 1927, and 1930. In 1926, he became the first player to notch victories in both the U.S. and British Open contests in the same year. In 1930, he rose to fame as the only player in history ever to win both national amateur and open tournaments in both countries.

Among Jones's many feats was a round of golf that has been described as being perfect as humanly possible. During the 1926 British Open, he shot a 66 (par was 72), divided evenly between going out and coming back. He tallied 6 fours and 3 threes on each nine, or 33 putts and 33 other strokes.

Jones did all of this as an amateur, often playing against the best professionals in the world. He was especially beloved by the golf-loving Scots.

After winning the Grand Slam in 1930, Jones retired from active competition. In 1934, he helped design the Augusta National Golf Course in Augusta, Georgia, and established the Masters Tournament that would be hosted there.

Jones was inducted into the Professional Golfers Association Hall of Fame in 1940. After his death in 1971, he was elected to the World Golf Hall of Fame.

A winner of a record six U.S. Women's Amateur titles, **GLENNA COLLETT VARE** did much to put women's golf on an equal "par" with the men's game.

Born in 1903 in Connecticut, Glenna Collett grew up in Providence, Rhode Island, as an accomplished athlete; she was proficient at swimming and diving as well as baseball and tennis. At fourteen, her father introduced her to golf at the Metacomet Golf Club in Providence.

Although she became quite good at the game, Collett played golf strictly for the enjoyment and the challenge. It was an attitude that she would keep for her entire life, despite her great success at the sport.

At the age of nineteen, she won the first of her six U.S. Women's Amateur Championships. In 1923 and 1924, she won the Canadian Ladies' Championship. Even after the Ladies' Professional Golf Association (LPGA) was formed, she retained her amateur standing because she did not want the tedium of playing every week. She recorded forty-nine amateur championships throughout her career and had nineteen consecutive victories between 1928 and 1931.

Becoming Collett Vare—she married **Edwin Vare** in her young adulthood—the golfer was often compared to **Bobby Jones** (see no. 17), who also only competed as an amateur. Jones once said of her: "It is especially a treat to watch Glenna Collett. Her accuracy with the spoon and brassie is to me the most important part of her well-rounded game."

Among Collett Vare's most famous accomplishments was winning her sixth U.S. Amateur title in 1935, after she had taken a two-year hiatus to start a family. She competed against younger stars such as **Marian McDougal**, **Betty Jameson**, and **Patty Berg** (see no. 26). The contest was her fourteenth national tournament.

Collett Vare continued to win tournaments at an age when most golfers would be retired, and she notched a victory in the Rhode Island State Championship at the age of fifty-six. Even when she was eighty, she maintained a fifteen handicap and competed in the Point Judith Invitational.

Glenna Collett Vare blazed a path that helped other women golfers succeed in what was once considered a male-dominated sport.

A legendary running back in college, **HAROLD EDWARD "RED" GRANGE** did more than almost any other player to put the National Football League (NFL) and professional football on the map for the public.

Born in Forksville, Pennsylvania, in 1903, Grange grew up in Wheaton, Illinois, where his family had moved when he was young. After high school—where he won sixteen letters in four sports—he enrolled at the University of Illinois (UI), where his exploits on the football field would gain him national recognition.

At UI, Grange became a terror on the gridiron. He was named to the All-American Team for three straight years from 1923–1925. In his college career, he averaged 5.3 yards per carry, scored thirty-one touchdowns, and threw six scoring passes.

Grange's most sensational day at UI came in 1924 in a game versus the school's traditional rival, the University of Michigan. At the time, Michigan had been unbeaten for twenty straight games. Grange rushed for 265 yards and four touchdowns—in the first twelve minutes of the game! In all, Grange scored five touchdowns the first five times he carried the ball, compiling 402 yards of total offense as Illinois rolled to victory, 39–14.

That game also saw Grange earn one of the most famous nicknames in sports history—the **Galloping Ghost**.

Grange left college immediately after his final game and joined the Chicago Bears of the NFL. His decision to play for the Bears before graduation day prompted a controversy that led to the adoption of the draft system, whereby a player had to graduate from college before he could sign with a pro team.

Despite missing several games with an injury and playing only briefly in others, Grange's time with the Bears was a great success. Unprecedented crowds came to games to watch Grange play, and he earned $100,000—the highest salary a pro football player had made up to that point. His presence gave the NFL sorely needed credibility and greatly helped pro football gain widespread acceptance with the public.

Grange then played two seasons with the New York Yankees in a newly formed American Football League after his initial season with the Bears, then returned to Chicago from 1929–1934. In 1933, he took part in the NFL's first championship game, in which the Bears beat New York, 23–21.

After his playing days ended, Grange became an assistant coach and later worked as a renowned radio and television football announcer. In 1961, he retired to Florida, where he had business interests. He died of pneumonia on January 28, 1991.

With nearly twenty major championship singles titles to her credit, **HELEN WILLS MOODY** was one of the greatest female tennis players in history.

She was born Helen Newington Wills in Centerville, California, and at her father's encouragement, she took up tennis as a youngster, mastering the game while she was just a teenager. She won the Pacific Coast Juniors at the age of fourteen and the National Juniors at fifteen. In 1922, at the age of sixteen, she reached the finals of the U.S. Championships in Forest Hills. The following year, she defeated **Molla Mallory** to win the title.

Wills developed a devastatingly powerful forehand shot, which she used to dominate women's tennis during the 1920s and 1930s. She won a gold medal in both singles and doubles at the 1924 Olympic Games; she is the only American woman to win an Olympic gold medal at tennis.

Wills graduated from the University of California in 1927, and two years later, she married **Frederick S. Moody**. She would compete over the next decade as Helen Wills Moody until the couple divorced in 1937. In 1939, she married **Aidan Roark**.

During her career, Wills Moody was in peak form at big tournaments. She won seven U.S. National singles championships from 1923–1925, again from 1927–1929, and lastly in 1931. She also won eight Wimbledon singles championships from 1927–1930, and then in 1932, 1933, 1935, and 1938—a record that was not broken until 1990. Wills Moody also claimed four French singles titles from 1928–1930, and in 1932, she played in ten Wightman Cup matches, winning eighteen out of twenty singles contests.

Called **Little Miss Poker Face** because of her unemotional style of play, Wills Moody also became known for bringing attention to athletic attire for female tennis players. Instead of long, heavy skirts and long sleeves, her typical outfit on the court was a white sailor suit, a white eyeshade, and white shoes with stockings.

In addition to her tennis career, Wills Moody was an author and an artist. Her autobiography, *Fifteen-Thirty: The Story of a Tennis Player*, was published in 1937, and she cowrote a mystery called *Death Serves an Ace* in 1939. Her drawings and paintings were displayed in several exhibitions in New York galleries.

SONJA HENIE changed the world of figure skating forever, turning a sport previously reserved for a few into one of widespread popularity.

Henie was born in Oslo, Norway, the second child of a fur merchant who indulged his children; she got her first pair of skates when she was eight years old. Henie quickly displayed so much ability on the ice that her father enrolled her in the best skating lessons.

In 1923, at the age of ten, she won the Norwegian National Championship. The following year, she competed in the Winter Olympics.

Henie was a natural athlete, who was good at many sports. She won the Scandinavian Championships in tennis and skiing, and also excelled in horseback riding, sprinting, and swimming.

However, it was figure skating that was destined to make Henie internationally famous. In 1927, she won the first of ten consecutive world championships. One year later, she won her first Olympic gold medal. She would win two more in 1932 and 1936. Overall, Henie won nearly 1,500 competitions throughout her career.

In 1936, Henie turned professional and became the featured performer in a touring ice show. She continued skating in ice shows well into the 1950s.

Henie also signed a movie contract in Hollywood with **Darryl F. Zanuck**, who ran the 20th Century Fox studio. The movies she made for Fox usually featured her skating and were highly successful.

Henie's skill and the success of her films helped popularize the sport of competitive figure skating. Ice rinks sprung up all over the Western Hemisphere, and a sport that had previously been the province of the rich or those in ice-bound countries suddenly enjoyed massive popularity around the world. Ice dancing became a popular pastime, and Henie's films inspired future Olympic champions like **Ludmila Beloussova** and **Oleg Protopopov** to don skates for the first time. (They won the gold medal in pairs skating in the 1964 and 1968 Olympics.)

Later in her career, Henie made ice skating specials for television. When she died of leukemia in 1969, it was estimated that she had made approximately $47 million from her various ventures. However, money aside, she will forever be remembered as the person who brought figure skating "in from the cold."

Born the son of a blacksmith in Dublin, Texas, **BEN HOGAN** rose from an extremely poor background to become one of the greatest golfers of all time.

After his father died when he was ten, Hogan had to sell newspapers to help keep the family fed. When he was twelve, Hogan switched to caddying at the Glen Garden Country Club in Fort Worth, and his career on the links was underway.

Hogan turned pro in 1931, and it took him several years to establish himself. However, by the early 1940s, he began to dominate the American golf scene and was the leading money-winner on the tour from 1940 to 1942.

He became known as a superb shot-maker, dubbed **the Hawk** by his competitors. Golfing great **Gene Sarazen** once said, "From tee to green, there never was anyone to compare with Hogan. If he had been able to putt as well as **Bobby Jones** (see no. 17) or **Jack Nicklaus** (see no. 46), no one could have come close to him. Yet he was such a

superb shotmaker that his putting was never put to too severe a test."

After he served in the Army Air Corps during World War II, Hogan rejoined the tour in 1945 and won thirty tournaments in the next four and a half years.

However, in February 1949, tragedy struck. Hogan and his wife were driving home to Fort Worth when a huge bus went out of control and careened into their lane. Instinctively, Hogan threw himself across the seat to protect his wife. His heroic action worked, as she suffered only minor injuries. But Hogan sustained a double fracture of the pelvis, a broken collarbone, a broken left ankle, and a broken rib.

It was feared that Hogan would have difficulty walking again. But the people who made that prediction had not counted on Hogan's iron will and determination. In January 1950, less than one year after the accident, Hogan battled **Sammy Snead** in the playoffs of the Los Angeles Open. A few months later, he won the U.S. Open title.

Nine months after his U.S. Open victory, Hogan won the 1951 Masters Tournament, and then won the U.S. Open again. In 1953, he won the Masters, the U.S. Open, and the British Open for a near Grand Slam. Altogether, from 1946 to 1953, Hogan won four U.S. Opens, two Masters, two Professional Golfers Association (PGA) tournaments, and the only British Open in which he ever competed.

Hogan was named PGA Player of the Year four times. After his retirement, he started a namesake golf manufacturing company.

WILLIE MOSCONI dominated the sport of pocket billiards in a way that had never been seen before and remains unprecedented today. Indeed, he is probably the greatest 14–1 straight pool champion the sport has ever known.

Born in Philadelphia in 1913, Mosconi was a child prodigy at billiards. His father owned a billiards parlor but wouldn't let his son play, so Mosconi would sneak in at night when he was five years old to practice with a broomstick and potatoes. Surprisingly, he then put down his cue stick and did not take it up again until 1931. Once he did, he established supremacy over the game.

Mosconi entered his first major tournament in 1937 and won his first world pocket billiards championship in 1941. He reigned champion again in 1942 and then from 1944–1948 and 1950–1955. When he retired from competition in 1957 after suffering a stroke, he still held the title.

During his career, Mosconi established a number of records, including exhibition high run with 527 balls, high run during a game with 127 balls, high run in tournament play with 150 balls, and most consecutive games won in tournament play with 14 victories.

Beginning in the 1950s, Mosconi began appearing in numerous public exhibitions that helped popularize the game of billiards. In 1954, he wrote a book, *Willie Mosconi on Pocket Billiards*, that further helped bring the game out of dank back rooms of bars and poolrooms and into mainstream American life. Over the years, he was a willing adviser to many young contenders as well. Impeccably dressed and possessing a scholarly attitude about the game, Mosconi established the image of a pocket billiards champion as having considerable finesse, skill, and class.

Mosconi served as a technical adviser to the 1961 Paul Newman/Jackie Gleason movie, *The Hustler*, a film that made pool shark **Minnesota Fats** (a.k.a. Rudolph Walderone) a household name. In 1978, Mosconi and "Fats" played an exhibition match featured on television, which Mosconi easily won.

Mosconi died of a heart attack in Haddon Heights, New Jersey, in 1993.

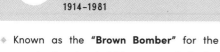

◆ Known as the **"Brown Bomber"** for the way he bombarded his opponents in the ring, **JOE LOUIS** was a great and memorable heavyweight champion.

He was born Joseph Louis Barrow near Lafayette, Alabama. He did odd jobs as a teenager and attended Bronson Vocational School before deciding he wanted to be a prizefighter.

Louis lost his first amateur bout, but quickly proved to be a formidable opponent in the ring. In 1934, he won the AAU Light Heavyweight Championship. He went on to record forty-three knockout victories in fifty-four fights as an amateur.

Turning pro, Louis won his initial fight with a first-round knockout on July 4, 1934, beating his opponent named **Jack Kraken**. Louis had twenty-five more fights from 1934–1935, beating such prominent heavyweights as former champions **Primo Carnera** and **Max Baer**.

The one fight that Louis lost, however, was in 1936 against German fighter **Max Schmeling**. It was a defeat that Nazi dictator

Adolf Hitler boasted about, claiming more evidence of his misguided philosophy of Aryan "racial superiority."

By the time Louis fought Schmeling in a rematch in 1938, the Brown Bomber had become the heavyweight champ by virtue of a victory over **James J. Braddock**. In front of a roaring crowd of 70,000 fans at Yankee Stadium in New York—and millions more listening via radio broadcast—Louis hammered Schmeling, knocking him out in just two minutes in the first round. The fight made Louis a national hero, as many saw it a victory for democracy over Nazi fascism and Hitler's repulsive racial theories.

As champion, Louis beat any and all comers, fighting so often in 1940–1941 that his opponents were jokingly dubbed the "Bum of the Month Club." He was not deterred by a faster man or a harder puncher, and he successfully defended his title thirty times over an eleven-year period from the late 1930s to the late 1940s. "He can run, but he can't hide," Louis said about one opponent, and the sentiment rang true for everyone he fought.

Louis enlisted in the army in 1942 and spent three years staging boxing exhibitions for U.S. soldiers, traveling some 21,000 miles to entertain troops.

Louis retired as the undefeated heavyweight champion in 1949. The following year, he returned to the ring, but the old magic was gone. He lost twice, including once by knockout at the hands of **Rocky Marciano** (see no. 28). Louis then permanently retired with a professional record of sixty-eight wins—fifty-four by knockout—and three losses.

Despite some financial problems with the government in his later years, Louis retained great popularity with the public until his death on April 12, 1981.

MARION LADEWIG is considered by many people to be the greatest female bowler of all time.

Ladewig was born in Grand Rapids, Michigan, in 1914. She began competing on the lanes as a young woman in her early twenties, long before the existence of a woman's professional bowling tour. In a way, Ladewig was lucky: the Michigan area where she grew up was home to some of the most competitive bowling in the country at that time. Ladewig fit right in, but soon, she would eclipse all her immediate competitors.

In 1944–1945, Ladewig had the highest bowling average in the United States, and it was a distinction she would earn three more times. In 1949, she became the first person to win the Bowling Proprietor's Association of America (BPAA) Woman's All-Star title. (It is now called the Women's U.S. Open.)

Then in 1950, Ladewig had one of the most spectacular years of any bowler in history. She won the Women's International Bowling Congress (WIBC) all-events title on the national level. She also won all-events titles on the city and state levels, becoming the only bowler in history to sweep the sport in such a manner.

As the years rolled on, so did Ladewig, often in spectacular fashion. In 1951, she maintained an eight-day average of 247.5. In 1955, she won the WIBC's all-events and doubles championships.

Ladewig has sometimes been compared to titans of other sports, such as **Babe Ruth** and **Gordie Howe** (see no. 32), and she certainly had the accomplishments to back up that comparison. She won the BPAA All-Star tournament eight times and the World Invitational title five times. She was a nine-time winner of the National Women Bowling Writers Association's American Woman Bowler of the Year award, which she won more than twice as often as any other woman in history.

Ladewig's popularity was such that she helped give rise to the Professional Women's Bowling Association. At the group's first professional tournament in 1960, Ladewig emerged victorious.

Ladewig placed third in the Associated Press's 1963 Woman Athlete of the Year poll. It was the first time that a bowler had ever made it that close to the top.

In 1964, Ladewig was inducted into the WIBC Hall of Fame. She retired in 1965, but still remained a force in the game by working as an adviser to the Brunswick Corporation, a bowling equipment manufacturer.

Interested in sports from when she was just a child, **PATTY BERG** grew up to become one of the leading female golfers of her era.

Born in Minneapolis, Minnesota, in 1918, Berg showed an affinity for sports as a teenager—only it wasn't golf, but football! She was the quarterback of the 50th Street Tigers, which, except for her, was an all-boys team. Her parents, deciding that she was too old to be involved in such activities, pointed her toward golf at the age of fourteen and bought her a membership at the Interlachen Country Club. One year later, she won the Minneapolis City Championship, and her amateur career was launched.

As an amateur, Berg rose to take the Minnesota state champion seat and won twenty-nine titles in seven years, including the 1938 U.S. Amateur title. She became widely recognized as the best and most famous female golfer in the United States.

It was inevitable that Berg would turn pro, which she did in 1940. Since there was no women's professional tour at the time, she earned a living by giving clinics and exhibitions. In 1941, she had a serious automobile accident, and was sidelined for more than a year.

When she returned to the game, Berg won the 1943 Western Open and All-American Open at Tam O'Shanter. She then joined the Marines. When she got out of the service, she won the 1946 U.S. Women's Open. She then became one of the founders of the LPGA and served as its first president from 1948–1952.

During the years from 1949–1960, Berg won thirty-nine LPGA tournaments. She was the leading money-winner among women golfers in 1954, 1955, and 1957. She was also a three-time winner of the Vare Trophy for the lowest average round in 1953, 1955, and 1956, and she was also named Female

Athlete of the Year by the Associated Press three times in 1938, 1943, and 1955. In 1952, she shot an LPGA 18-hole record of 64. Throughout her career, Berg qualified for every tournament she ever entered—a record she still holds.

In 1951, when she was one of the first four golfers inducted into the LPGA Hall of Fame, Berg said, "I'm very happy that I gave up football, or I wouldn't be here tonight." In 1978, she became one of the first two women inducted into the PGA Hall of Fame.

The first African American to win an Olympic weightlifting championship, **JOHN DAVIS** in his prime was known as the **"Strongest Man in the World."**

Born in Brooklyn, New York, in 1921, Davis displayed his tremendous strength when he was young. At the age of seventeen, he won the light heavyweight world championship in Vienna. He then began an amazing streak in which he was undefeated in all competitions between 1938 and 1953. During this time, he broke nineteen world records and won twelve national titles and a gold medal at the Pan American Games.

In 1941, before middle heavyweight became an officially recognized weight class, Davis completed lifts of 322.25 pounds in the press, 317.5 pounds in the snatch, and a clean and jerk of 370 pounds. This added up to the extraordinary total of 1009.75 pounds. Davis went on to become a full-fledged heavyweight. His best individual lifts

were 342 pounds in the press, 330.5 pounds in the snatch, and 402 pounds in the clean and jerk. Davis could curl 215 pounds and bench press 425. He once performed a two-handed dead lift of 705 pounds.

Davis is one of only twelve weightlifters ever to have won two Olympic championships. At the 1948 Olympics, Davis lifted 137.5 kg in the press and snatch, and 177 kg in the jerk for a total of 314.5 kg. He returned to the Games in 1952 in Helsinki, Finland, and lifted a total of 460 kg: 150 in the press, 145 in the snatch, and 165 in the jerk.

Davis was world champion six times in his weight classification, and from 1948–1956, he won thirty-two state, national, Olympic, and world weightlifting championships. He was the world's amateur heavyweight champion in 1946, 1947, 1949, 1950, and 1951.

In 1952, Davis was the subject of the first Olympic-related film made by noted sports filmmaker **Bud Greenspan**. It was called, appropriately enough, *The Strongest Man in the World*.

Davis's last appearance on the lifting platform was not a happy one. During the 1956 Olympic trials, he tore a ligament in his knee attempting to clean nearly 400 pounds and had to be carried off the stage on a stretcher.

In an age when African American athletes were struggling for recognition, John Davis helped greatly raise their visibility.

ROCKY MARCIANO, a.k.a. the "**Brockton Blockbuster**," was one of the greatest heavyweight champions of all time. Flinging the thunderous right hook that he called the "Susie Q," Marciano compiled a record of 49–0, retiring as the only undefeated heavyweight champion in boxing history.

Born Rocco Francis Marchegiano in Brockton, Massachusetts, he began fighting in the U.S. Army when he was twenty years old. After he got out, he continued fighting under an assumed name, **Rocky Mack**, to preserve his amateur status. He won all his amateur fights except one.

When Marciano turned pro in 1947, he quickly proved that he was going to be a force—only two of his first nine opponents lasted beyond the first round. He was a paradox in many ways, savagely pummeling his opponents on the one hand, then feeling guilty for winning the bout. In 1951, after pounding former champion **Joe Louis**, Marciano wept, and later sent the ex-champ a note telling him how sorry he was that the fight had turned out the way it did. When a boxer named **Carmine Vingo** was left paralyzed from the waist down after a fight with Marciano, Rocky paid the $2,000 for his hospital bills.

With his straight-ahead, relentless pounding style, Marciano faced technical wizard **Jersey Joe Walcott** for the heavyweight title in September 1952. Walcott knocked Marciano down in the first round, and for two full rounds he was blinded by medication that had been put on one of his facial cuts. Yet Marciano survived, and in the thirteenth round, he landed his devastating right hook and knocked Walcott out.

Marciano went on to defend his title five more times over the next several years, including a first-round knockout of Walcott in their rematch and two defeats of former champion **Ezzard Charles**. One fight with Charles went fifteen rounds—the only fifteen-round fight of Marciano's career.

On September 21, 1955, Marciano met light heavyweight champion **Archie Moore** in a fight that has been called one of the greatest bouts in boxing history.

The two men often stood toe-to-toe in the ring, throwing punches at each other with wild abandon, all semblance of strategy or style forgotten. Finally, Marciano KO'd the still-game but exhausted Moore in the ninth round.

It was Marciano's last fight. He retired in April 1956, partly at the urging of his mother. In 1969, he participated in a series of fight sequences with **Muhammad Ali** that were fed into a computer to determine the greatest heavyweight of all time. Marciano won by a thirteenth-round knockout.

Marciano died in a plane crash on August 31, 1969.

Professional basketball's first superstar **GEORGE MIKAN** was the first dominant big man in the National Basketball Association (NBA). Although his time in the league was relatively brief, he left a lasting impact on the game, and his career foreshadowed the emergence of great NBA centers such as **Bill Russell** (see no. 40) and **Wilt Chamberlain** (see no. 42).

George Mikan was born in 1924 in Joliet, Illinois. He didn't play basketball in high school because he was awkward, and a badly broken leg kept him recovering at home for a year and a half. In 1942, he entered DePaul University in Chicago, as a 6-foot-10, 245-pound freshman who wore thick glasses.

At DePaul, under the coaching of **Ray Meyer**, Mikan not only learned the game of basketball—he became a great player. Meyer taught Mikan the fundamentals as well as how to make hook shots with either hand. For three years, Mikan reigned as a three-time all-American from 1944–1946,

and College Player of the Year in 1945 and 1946. He also led DePaul to the 1945 National Invitational Tournament title.

After school, Mikan joined the professional Chicago American Gears of the National Basketball League. He led the Gears to the National Baseball League (NBL) championship in 1947, and after the Gears folded, Mikan joined the NBL's Minneapolis Lakers, with whom he was to reach stardom.

In 1948, the NBL and the Basketball Association of America merged to form the NBA. Mikan led the new league in scoring its first three years and led the Lakers to five league championships—in 1949, 1950, and from 1952–1954—in six years. He was such a dominant player that he was sometimes guarded by two or even three defenders.

During his career, Mikan was named to the All-Star team six consecutive seasons, averaged 22.6 points per game, and scored 11,764 points in 520 games; his average in postseason play was 23.5.

Mikan was such a dominating force in the sport that, in 1950, the Associated Press selected him by poll as the greatest basketball player of the first half of the twentieth century.

Mikan retired after the 1956 season, then came back to coach the Lakers for one year. When the American Basketball Association was formed in 1967, he became its first commissioner—a position he held until he resigned in 1969. As commissioner, Mikan came up with the league's unique red, white, and blue multicolored ball.

Mikan was part of the first class elected to the Basketball Hall of Fame in 1959. In 1996, he was named on the NBA's 50 Greatest Players list for the league's 50th Anniversary Team.

With great skill and tireless promotion of his sport, **DONALD JAMES CARTER** indeed lived up to his nickname as "**Mr. Bowling**."

Born on July 29, 1926, in St. Louis, Missouri, Carter was a two-sports star in high school, but neither sport, ironically, was bowling. At that time, baseball and football were his standout sports. Carter entered the U.S. Navy during World War II, and after being discharged, he played one season of minor league baseball as pitcher and infielder. He then returned to St. Louis to manage a bowling center.

Once the man and the sport finally met, Carter quickly established his mastery over the game of bowling. His unusual right-handed backswing gave him an advantage over his opponents. He won the Bowling Proprietors' Association of America All-Star Tournament (today, the BPAA U.S. Open) for the first time in 1953. He would go on to win it three more times in 1954, 1957, and 1958. The Professional Bowlers Association (PBA) was formed in 1958, and Carter won the group's first championship tournament in 1960 with a score of 6,512 for thirty games. The following year, he won the American Bowling Congress (ABC) Masters Tournament with an average score of 211.18.

Carter was voted Bowler of the Year six times—in 1953, 1954, 1957, 1958, 1960, and 1962. The final year, he led the PBA tour in earnings with $22,525 and in overall average with a score of 212.84. Carter led the PBA in earnings again with $49,972 in 1964. That same year, he signed a $1 million dollar contract from bowling ball manufacturer Ebonite International to endorse their bowling products, and became the first athlete in any sport to receive a single endorsement deal of that high value. He capitalized on his celebrity by bringing attention to his sport through televised events.

In 1970, a *Bowling Magazine* poll named him the best bowler of all time. He retired from competitive play two years later, but continued to play for fun at his own national chain of bowling alleys. He is a member of the Hall of Fame of both the ABC and PBA.

BOB COUSY was known for his phenomenal play-making ability, which revolutionized basketball. He also was a big part of the fabled Boston Celtics dynasty of the late 1950s and 1960s.

The son of French immigrants, Robert Joseph Cousy was born in New York City in 1928 and spoke only French until he was six years old. His family moved to St. Albans, Queens, when he was twelve, and when he was in junior high school, he began experimenting with ballhandling—behind-the-back passes and other techniques that would fool the opposition. Cousy did not make junior varsity in high school until his sophomore year, and in his junior year, he was not allowed to play until January. Nevertheless, in a full senior-year season, he led the city in scoring and was named to the all-city team.

Cousy attended Holy Cross College on a basketball scholarship. As a freshman, he played on a National Collegiate Athletic Association (NCAA) championship team and was an all-American athlete in his senior year. Nicknamed the **"Houdini of the Hardwood,"** his brilliant ballhandling influenced the entire team.

Ironically, although Cousy is associated most strongly with the Boston Celtics, the team had initially passed up the chance to draft him. He was taken instead by the Tri-Cities Blackhawks and then went to the Chicago American Gears.

When the Gears folded, Cousy's name was put into a hat along a few other straggler teammates. The Celtics picked his name, and years later legendary coach **Red Auerbach** marveled, "We got stuck with the greatest player in the league when we drew his name out of a hat."

In his thirteen seasons with the Celtics from 1950–1963, Cousy helped them win six NBA championships—one in 1957 and five consecutively from 1959–1963. Teaming up with defensive genius **Bill Russell** (see no. 40), Cousy helped build up the Celtics as one of the true dynasties in professional sports.

Individually, Cousy led the league in assists eight times and was chosen for the NBA All-Star Team every season he was with the Celtics. In a 1953 playoff game, Cousy made ten field goals and a playoff record 30 of 32 free throws, for a total of 50 points. He was named the league's Most Valuable Player (MVP) in 1957, which was the first time the Celtics had won the championship.

Cousy retired after the 1963 season at the age of thirty-four, leaving Russell and others to continue the Celtics' winning tradition. When he quit, Cousy ranked first in the league in career assists and third in scoring.

After his retirement, Cousy coached at Boston College for six seasons and then coached the NBA's Cincinnati Royals (later the Kansas City Omaha Kings) for several seasons.

GORDIE HOWE's nickname says it all: "**Mr. Hockey**." In a career that spanned more than thirty years, Howe set numerous National Hockey League (NHL) scoring records and was named the league's MVP six times.

Howe was born in Floral, Saskatchewan, Canada, but his family soon moved to nearby Saskatoon, where Howe learned to play hockey on a rink in the family backyard, swapping out his tennis ball for a puck.

He was so proficient at the game that, by the time he was fifteen, he was already being pursued by teams from the NHL. At sixteen, he was signed by the Detroit Red Wings, who sent him to the minor leagues.

When he was eighteen, Howe joined the Red Wings, where he played steady but unspectacular hockey for the first three seasons. However, in the 1949 Stanley Cup playoffs, he notched eight goals and three assists—a total unmatched by any other player that year.

That series seemed to ignite something in Howe. He went on to lead the NHL in scoring for four straight years from 1951–1954—and

six times overall. With his matchless stick-handling and shooting from either side of his body, few could keep up. In addition to being a prolific scorer, Howe was an outstanding defensive player who averaged nearly twice the playing time on the ice of most forwards.

Howe was an ageless wonder who seemed as if he might play hockey forever. On his twenty-fifth anniversary with the Red Wings, NHL coaches named him "The smartest player, best passer, best playmaker, and best puck carrier" in the league. By that time, Howe's sons Mark and Marty were also playing for Detroit.

Shortly thereafter, though, the Red Wings made the mistake of taking Howe off the ice and putting him in a front-office job. Howe and his sons quickly departed for the Houston club of the new World Hockey Association (WHA). He led Houston to the league championship in 1972, proving that there was plenty of life left in his hockey legs.

Howe won the WHA's MVP Award in 1974 and led Houston to another championship in 1975. He and his sons then signed with the WHA's Hartford Whalers, who joined the NHL in 1977, and Howe continued to play for them until he retired in 1980 at the remarkable age of fifty-two.

When Howe retired, he led the NHL in career goals and total points scored. He is now second to **Wayne Gretzky** (see no. 77) in both categories. Howe also ranks among the career leaders in Stanley Cup playoff goals, assists, and points.

The pillar of the Montreal Canadiens' dynasty in the late 1950s and the first goalie to wear a protective mask, **JACQUES PLANTE** significantly influenced the sport of hockey.

Plante was an asthmatic child living in Mont-Carmel, Quebec, Canada when he began playing hockey as a young boy. He became so good that, by age twenty, he was a prominent minor league player for the Montreal Royals. He got his big break in the 1953 Stanley Cup semifinals, when the Montreal Canadiens needed him to replace their regular goaltender. Plante sparkled for the two games he played, allowing just one goal and leading Montreal to the finals. In that series, he split goaltending duties with the team's regular goalie. The Canadiens beat the Boston Bruins to win the Stanley Cup.

Installed the following season as the Canadiens' regular goalie, Plante rapidly established himself as the leading netkeeper in the entire NHL. He led the league in shutouts three straight years from 1956–1958 and in goals-against average from 1956–1960—and again in 1962. During that time, the Canadiens won five straight Stanley Cups from 1956–1960. Plante was voted the NHL's MVP in 1961.

Plante was an innovator in the crease. He developed the now-common technique of moving out of the goal area with the puck still in play in order to stop a rush by the other team or to break up their play. Conversely, he was not shy about moving out of the crease to aid his own team's efforts.

However, his biggest innovation came when he began wearing a molded plastic mask to protect himself. He started doing this after he was injured in the face by a rocketing puck. While goalies had worn plastic masks to protect themselves during practices, Plante was the first to do so during games. Soon after, all goalies followed suit to protect themselves from the hard rubber pucks.

Plante retired in 1965 but came back with the St. Louis Blues in 1967. Proving that age had not diminished his skills, he once again led the NHL in goals-against average in the 1967–1968 season.

After several seasons in the WHA, Plante finally retired for good in 1975 at the age of forty-five. He finished his career as a seven-time winner of the Goaltender of the Year Award, with 82 shutouts and a 2.38 goals-against average. In 1978, he was elected to the NHL Hall of Fame.

Sometimes sports heroes and star athletes are the most unlikely of people. That is certainly the case with **SIR ROGER BANNISTER**, a mild-mannered English medical student who became the first man in history to run a mile in less than four minutes.

For hundreds of years, it was considered impossible to run a mile in under four minutes. Even the greatest runners in the history of the sport, such as **Paavo Nurmi** (see no. 16), could never break the four-minute barrier. However, in 1952, Australian runner **John Landy** made it known that the four-minute mile was his goal. He came close, clocking a time of 4:02.

At the same time, Roger Bannister was studying Landy's runs, convinced that he could do better.

Bannister was born in Harrow, England, and was educated at Oxford. As a runner, he had much in common with Nurmi. Like that great track star, Bannister believed that he could better his time through intensive training, combined with a careful analysis of running conditions, pacing, timed acceleration, and other factors. He knew that he would have to run four laps around the track while averaging slightly less than sixty seconds per lap to achieve his goal.

In May 1953, after intensive training, he put his theory to the test. He ran the first two laps too slowly, but still set a new British mile record of 4:03.6.

When John Landy subsequently ran a 4:02 mile and declared that he had hit "a brick wall," Bannister knew that the four-minute record was his for the taking. He stepped up his training from December 1953 through the spring of 1954. He circled May 6 on his calendar. On that date, Oxford would have a meet with the British Amateur Athletic Association, and he was determined to go for the record at that event.

Bannister trained rigorously for weeks and then rested a few days before the event to conserve his energy. When the big day came, Bannister ran the first quarter in 57.5 seconds, and at the half-mile mark, his split was 1:58. His three-quarter mile time was 3:00.5, and he broke the tape at 3:59.4—a new world record.

Just over a month later, Landy beat Bannister's mark, clocking a 3:58 mile. In June 1954, the two men competed against each other at the British Commonwealth Games. Ironically, both men recorded times of less than four minutes, though neither set a world record. Bannister won the race.

Bannister's last win in international competition was in the 1,500-meter race in the European Games in 1954. He subsequently retired from running to practice medicine. He was knighted in 1975.

ARNOLD PALMER came along just as televised sports were growing in popularity, and golf in particular was reaching a greater audience than ever before. The face of golf on television became the face of the personable and talented Palmer, who became the first golfer to earn more than $1 million in prize money.

Palmer was born in Latrobe, Pennsylvania, to a father who was a greens keeper and pro on the local golf course. Showing an early interest in the game, Palmer began playing golf when he was three years old and became a caddie at the age of eleven. In 1946, he entered his first national golf tournament when he was seventeen.

Then his career was interrupted by tragedy. His best friend was killed in an automobile accident, and a distraught Palmer joined the Coast Guard. When he was discharged in 1953, he became a sales representative.

However, he could not fully abandon golf. In 1954, he won the National Amateur Championship, and made a life-altering decision to turn pro. For several years, he and his wife scrambled to survive financially, but Palmer's income grew as his golf game improved. In 1958, he led the PGA with $42,607 in winnings.

Palmer was at his best in big tournaments. He won four Masters Tournaments in 1958, 1960, 1962, and 1964—and the British Open twice in 1961 and 1962. Sometimes his victories came in spectacular fashion. In 1960, he was fourteenth going into the final round at the U.S. Open. He birdied six of the first seven holes, posted a record-tying tournament score of 30 for the first nine holes, and finished the second nine with 35. His 65 was the lowest final round ever shot by a U.S. Open winner up to that time.

In 1963, Palmer won more than $125,000, and by 1968, he had become the first golfer to earn more than $1 million in prize money. However, Palmer not only won a lot of tournaments and prize money, he is credited with almost single-handedly popularizing golf during the 1960s. With his large fan following known as "Arnie's Army," and his "everyman" demeanor, he brought golf into the television age and introduced the game to a whole legion of at-home viewers.

In 1980, Palmer joined the senior tour and immediately won the Seniors Championship that year. Then he won it again in 1984. Throughout the 1980s, he continued his winning ways on the senior tour.

With his various business interests, Palmer remained quite visible in the public well after he retired from the game. To millions of fans, he will always be the face of professional golf.

A member of the U.S. Olympic Hall of Fame, **PAT MCCORMICK** is the only female diver to win two gold medals in two consecutive Olympics.

Born Patricia Keller in 1930 in Seal Beach, California, she took to the water at an early age and proved herself by winning the Long Beach One-Meter Gold Cup at the age of fourteen. After graduating from high school, she attended California State University at Long Beach. In 1949, she married Glenn McCormick.

McCormick won her first national championship at the national outdoor platform dive in 1949. She won the same event four more times in 1950, 1951, 1954, and 1955. She also won the outdoor one-meter and three-meter springboard championships six times in 1950, 1951, and then straight through from 1953–1956.

McCormick was just as dominant indoors. She won the one-meter springboard five consecutive years beginning in 1951 and the three-meter in 1951, 1952, 1954, and 1955.

McCormick first gained international recognition in 1951 by winning the ten-meter platform event at the Pan American Games. However, it was in the following year that the world really took notice when she won gold medals in both the springboard and platform events at the 1952 Summer Olympics in Helsinki, Finland.

McCormick continued her international success at the 1955 Pan American Games, again winning the springboard and platform events. The following year, she gave birth to a son, but she came back to show that childbirth had not affected her athletic skills. Eight months later, she won gold medals again in both the springboard and platform events at the 1956 Olympics in Melbourne, Australia, becoming the first diver to win both events in two back-to-back Olympics.

Early in her career, McCormick often performed difficult dives usually attempted only by men and which were illegal to perform in international competition until 1952. McCormick's daily Olympic training regimen included a two-and-a-half-hour drill on a 33-foot-high platform, then two hours of springboard practice plus a three-hour evening workout, totaling 80 to 100 dives per day, six days a week. It was her way of fine-tuning her skills by demanding more from herself than she would ever need.

Following her incredible Olympic performance in 1956, McCormick won the James E. Sullivan Award that year as outstanding amateur athlete in the United States. After her triumphs in the 1956 Olympics, McCormick retired from competition and operated a diving camp for years.

In 1984, McCormick joined the escort group for the American flag at the opening ceremonies of the Olympics, where her daughter Kelly won silver in the springboard event.

BILL SHOEMAKER is known as **"Mr. Horse Racing."** When he retired in 1990, he had 8,833 career victories—the most in the history of all jockeys.

Ironically, the greatest jockey in history was not expected to survive his own birth. A premature baby born on a cotton farm near Fabens, Texas, he weighed just two and a half pounds when he came into the world, and doctors were skeptical that he would make it. However, his grandmother nurtured him in a shoe box she placed in front of the door of a warm oven, and Shoemaker overcame his gloomy prognosis and grew up healthy.

He weighed eighty-five pounds in high school and had tremendous strength for someone his size. He once won a boxing competition against boys of 100 pounds and over.

Reasoning that the best place for boys his size was on the racetrack, Shoemaker worked as a groom and exercise boy at a ranch. He saved enough money to go to California and learn to be an exercise rider. When a trainer saw him working with and riding the animals, he was impressed enough to put him into his first race.

Shoemaker did not win that first race, but he did win his third. In fact, in his first year alone, Shoemaker won 219 times. The next year, he won 388 times. In his third year, he set an all-time record with 485 wins.

Thereafter, there was no stopping the four-foot-eleven, 103-pound Shoemaker. He won the Belmont Stakes five times in 1957, 1959, 1962, 1967, and 1975; the Kentucky Derby four times in 1955, 1959, 1965, and 1986; and the Preakness twice in 1963 and 1967. He was the leading money-winner among jockeys for seven consecutive years from 1958–1964. In 1986, he became the oldest jockey to ever win the Kentucky Derby.

Between 1949 and 1990, Shoemaker rode in more than 40,250 races—more than any other jockey in history. He won more than $123 million in purses, another all-time record.

Shoemaker's racing style was as unique as the man himself. Prior to a race, he studied each horse's history and its wins and losses, trying to discern the motivations behind peak performance. He used the whip sparingly and often hung back at the beginning of a race. He waited until his opponents had made their moves before he passed them. These techniques often helped him achieve surprising results out of underrated horses.

In 1990, Shoemaker retired from racing to become a horse trainer. In 1991, he suffered a devastating automobile accident that left him paralyzed, but showing his indomitable spirit, he continued to work with his beloved horses.

Every struggling football player should be required to learn about the career of **JOHNNY UNITAS**. Overlooked, underestimated, and then cut from his first pro team, he persevered and went on to become perhaps the greatest quarterback in NFL history.

Unitas was born in Pittsburgh, Pennsylvania, and went to college at the University of Louisville. He played quarterback there but was virtually unknown nationally. Unitas's dream was to play pro football for his hometown Pittsburgh Steelers, and he initially got that chance after he was the Steelers' ninth-round draft choice in 1955. However, even though they were a sad-sack NFL team at that time, they were unimpressed with Unitas. He was afforded virtually no playing time in training camp as a rookie, and the team cut him before the next season began.

Discouraged but not defeated, Unitas hooked up the following year with the Baltimore Colts. Before long, he was the team's starting quarterback.

The NFL did not have the wide television exposure then that it has today. There was no Monday Night Football and even Sunday telecasts were sparse as the twelve NFL teams that televised their games only broadcast regionally. However, in 1958, Unitas quarterbacked the Colts to a thrilling 23–17 overtime victory against the New York Giants in the NFL Championship game, a contest televised on national TV. Called by many the greatest pro football game ever played, the event firmly established the NFL as an institution in the homes of sports fans everywhere.

Unitas again led the Colts to victory over the Giants in the 1959 Championship game. He was voted MVP in both games. For much of the next decade, Unitas was in his prime. He was voted Player of the Year three times in 1959, 1964, and 1967; led the league in touchdown passes four straight years from 1957–1960; and also led in passing yardage four times. He additionally had three seasons in which he threw 3,000 yards or more and was a ten-time pro.

During Unitas's era, quarterbacks called their own plays rather than the coaches, and Unitas was considered the most brilliant play-caller of the time. The great coach **Vince Lombardi** said of him, "He is uncanny in his abilities, under the most violent pressure, to pick out the soft spot in a defense."

When he retired after the 1974 season, Unitas had a total of 40,239 career passing yards and 290 touchdown passes. He was elected to the Pro Football Hall of Fame in 1979, and he was named the quarterback of the NFL's All-Time Team in 2000 by Hall of Fame voters.

LARISA LATYNINA was the first female athlete to win nine gold medals at the Olympics, and her amazing success helped popularize gymnastics all over the world.

She was born in 1934 in Kherson, in the present-day country of Ukraine, which at the time was part of the Soviet Union. As a child, Latynina trained as a ballet dancer, where her exceptional balance and poise were readily apparent. She went on to formal education at the Kiev State Institute of Physical Culture and was a national school gymnastic champion at the age of sixteen.

Latynina burst onto the international stage at the 1956 Olympics. There she won the individual All-Around Olympic Championship with a score of 74.933 and tied for first in the floor exercise with 18.733 points.

She also won the vault event and helped lead the Soviet team to victory in the combined competition.

Latynina routed the opposition at the 1957 and 1958 European championships, winning five individual events. In 1958, she reigned as world champion on the uneven bars, the balance beam, and the vault.

Latynina then shone again at the 1960 Olympics, winning the floor exercise outright with a score of 19.583, and again taking the all-around championship with a score of 77.031. Again, she helped lead the Soviets to victory in the overall team competition.

Two years later, she once more won an all-around championship and was the world champion in the floor exercise. At the 1964 Olympics, she was victorious again in the floor exercise with a total of 19.599 points, while leading the Soviet team to another all-around victory.

Across her three Olympics, in addition to her record nine gold medals, Latynina also won five silver and four bronze medals. Her eighteen Olympic medals made her the all-time overall leading medal winner. Latynina's astonishing career helped put kids on the parallel bars and the rings all over the world. In her homeland, she blazed a path for future gymnastics stars to walk, such as **Olga Korbut**.

After she retired, Latynina became a coach for the Soviet gymnastic team and helped plan the 1980 Moscow Olympics.

He teamed with **Bob Cousy** to turn the Boston Celtics into a perennial NBA champion, and his battles with **Wilt Chamberlain** were legendary. He was defensive genius **BILL RUSSELL**, one of the most dominant figures in the history of basketball.

Russell was born in Monroe, Louisiana, in 1934, and suffered a great deal of racial discrimination as a child. The experience made him that more assertive about African American rights as an adult. His family moved to Oakland, California, where Russell made his high school basketball team as a junior. At six-foot-two, he was somewhat awkward and was only a third string player.

It was as a college player that Russell garnered national attention. He attended the University of San Francisco where, as a six-foot-nine sophomore, he became the team's starting center. Along with **K. C. Jones**, Russell turned the school into a basketball powerhouse. The team won fifty-five consecutive games at one point and won back-to-back NCAA titles in 1955 and 1956.

After helping the U.S. team take home the gold in the 1956 Olympics, Russell was drafted by the NBA's Boston Celtics. There, along with play-making genius Bob Cousy, he turned the team into a basketball juggernaut.

Russell added the necessary defensive ingredients—mainly shot-blocking and rebounding—to Cousy's play-making wizardry to turn the Celtics into an unstoppable force. Boston won the NBA championship in Russell's first year, finished second the following season, then reeled off a run of eight straight titles beginning in 1959.

Russell was voted the NBA's MVP four times in 1958, 1961, 1962, and 1963. He had 21,620 career rebounds, averaged more than twenty-two rebounds per game, and led the league in rebounding four times. He also scored more than 14,000 points in his career.

Russell and the great **Wilt Chamberlain** (see no. 42) were the two most dominating players in the league during the 1960s, and their battles on the hard court were classic. While Chamberlain was an unstoppable offensive force, Russell was a better rebounder and shot-blocker. Aided by a much better supporting cast, the Celtics usually came out on top in their head-to-head battles.

In 1966, Russell became the first African American coach in major professional sports when he was tapped as player-coach of the Celtics. He then led them to back-to-back championships in 1968 and 1969. In Russell's career, he won eleven NBA titles over thirteen seasons—a record that will almost certainly never be surpassed.

Russell subsequently coached the NBA's Seattle Supersonics and Sacramento Kings, and he was elected to the Basketball Hall of Fame in 1974.

The first four-time winner of the Indianapolis 500, **ANTHONY JOSEPH "A. J." FOYT** is one of the all-time greats in the history of auto racing.

Foyt was born in Houston, Texas, with gasoline in his veins. His father was a garage owner, midget car racer, and mechanical genius. He could wring every available foot-pound of horsepower from a gasoline engine.

The young Foyt won his first race at the age of five, in a car his dad built. Thoroughly bitten by the racing bug, he left high school to become a mechanic and begin his racing career. He was so good that he dominated the tracks where he lived. He moved onto the Midwest at the age of eighteen, driving against the big names in auto racing in the 1950s. It didn't matter to Foyt what type of car he drove—sprints, midgets, stocks—as long as he could race them.

That type of burning, competitive desire gave Foyt a reputation that he carried with him when he joined the United States Auto Club (USAC) in preparation for racing in the Indianapolis 500. His first USAC event was driving a midget racer in 1956.

In 1958, Foyt qualified for the 500. He drove in the prestigious race in one of the legendary Dean Van Lines Specials and finished sixteenth.

Three years later, Foyt won his first Indy 500—a feat he would repeat in 1964, 1967, and 1977, setting new speed records with the first two victories.

In his career, Foyt won seven USAC championships in 1960, 1961, 1963, 1964, 1967, 1975, and 1979. Among the major races he has won are the 1972 Daytona 500 and the 24 Hours of Le Mans in 1967. He also won the 24 Hours of Daytona twice in 1983 and 1985.

Foyt had a unique career in auto racing in that he drove virtually every type of car except for professional drag racers. He also continued to enjoy considerable success as he got older, although auto racing is typically a young man's sport.

Despite suffering injuries several times in crashes over the years, Foyt continued his legendary career until 1993. Fittingly, he announced his retirement during the qualifying trials for the Indianapolis 500.

WILT CHAMBERLAIN was an unstoppable force in basketball. Although he never achieved the type of championship success that **Bill Russell** (see no. 40) did, Chamberlain is nevertheless remembered as perhaps the most dominating offensive presence the game has ever seen.

Born in Philadelphia to his parents of average size, Chamberlain reached a height of six feet by the age of ten. In school, he wanted to be a track-and-field star and dreamed of competing in the Olympics as a sprinter. However, he was nearly seven feet tall when he was in high school, and his height literally compelled him to play basketball. He led his team at Philadelphia's Overbrook High School to three public school championships and two all-city titles.

Not surprisingly, every college in the country vied for Chamberlain, and the University of Kansas was the winner. Over his two-year college career, he averaged 29.9 points and 18.3 rebounds per game. He was named College Player of the Year in 1957.

Chamberlain left college after his junior year to play with the Harlem Globetrotters for one season. In 1959, he was selected by the NBA's Philadelphia Warriors in the draft, and the seven-foot-one, 275-pound giant immediately turned that team into an NBA powerhouse. He averaged 37.6 points and twenty-seven rebounds during his first season, earning both Rookie of the Year and MVP honors.

By his third season in 1961–1962, Chamberlain was reaching nearly unimaginable heights as a player. He averaged an astonishing 50.4 points that season with 25.7 rebounds. On March 2, 1962, he had perhaps the greatest individual game in NBA history as he poured in 100 points when the Warriors defeated the New York Knicks 169–147. Chamberlain scored 31 points in the final period alone.

However, despite his individual success, Chamberlain's couldn't lead his team to an NBA title, generating charges that he wasn't a team player and couldn't win the big games. His battles under the basket with Bill Russell of the Celtics were classic, but Russell, who benefited from a better supporting cast of players, almost always emerged victorious. Finally, in 1967, playing for the Philadelphia 76ers with other talented players, Chamberlain earned his first championship.

Traded in 1968 to the Los Angeles Lakers, Chamberlain again shared the scoring spotlight with other great players, such as **Jerry West**. In 1972, the Lakers had one of their greatest seasons in history, and Chamberlain got another championship. After that, he played one more season, and then retired.

Chamberlain left the game with numerous records, including most points at 31,419 and most rebounds at 23,924. In 1978, he was elected to the Basketball Hall of Fame.

JIM BROWN
b. 1936

JIM BROWN played professional football for only nine seasons, but during that time, he managed to become perhaps the greatest running back in NFL history.

Born in 1936 on St. Simon's Island, Georgia, Brown eventually moved to the New York City area when he was seven. An excellent high school athlete in several sports, he was considered one of the best school athletes in New York history.

Brown's fiercely independent streak surfaced when he chose to attend Syracuse University (SU), one of the few colleges that had not offered him an athletic scholarship. (He was offered a total of forty-two athletic scholarships.) A good friend who wanted him to succeed crowdfunded money from a group of Jim Brown fans to finance his way to college.

At SU, Brown won ten varsity letters: two in track and baseball each, and three in lacrosse and football each. He was an all-American athlete in lacrosse and football.

After he graduated, Brown turned down a $150,000 offer to become a professional fighter. Instead, he joined the NFL after the Cleveland Browns drafted him for the 1957 season. Brown was Rookie of the Year that season, in which he gained 942 yards on 202 carries. In one game against the Los Angeles Rams, he set a rushing record of 237 yards, scoring four touchdowns as well.

Over the next eight seasons, Brown was virtually unstoppable as he rampaged through the rest of the NFL. He scored a record 126 career touchdowns, led the league in rushing yardage seven times, and was named to the All-Pro Team eight times. On top of all that, he was also MVP twice.

At six-foot, two-inches tall and 228 pounds, Brown combined excellent speed with elusive moves. While he rarely ran over an opponent, his speed and power allowed him to break many off-balance tackles.

Brown rushed for over 1,000 yards in seven seasons, over 200 yards in a game four times, and over 100 yards in a game fifty-four times. Remarkably, he never sat out due to injury. Even more surprising, Brown established his rushing marks in seasons that contained twelve or at most fourteen games. In 1963, Brown became the first football player to gain more than a mile in a season when he rushed for a total of 1,863 yards.

No one knows what other rushing records he could have set, but Brown retired at the conclusion of the 1966 season to pursue an acting career. He finished with 12,312 lifetime yards—the most in NFL history at the time. He was voted into the Pro Football Hall of Fame in 1971.

The first stock car driver to win $1 million in prize money, **RICHARD PETTY** retired as the all-time leader in victories on the professional stock car circuit.

Born in North Carolina, Petty grew up in the world of auto racing, much like **A. J. Foyt** (see no. 41). His father was **Lee Petty**, an early National Association of Stock Car Auto Racing (NASCAR) champion. The younger Petty often said that he became a race car driver because his father was one, and because he enjoyed the entire auto racing environment.

Petty began his career as a mechanic for his father, and he first got behind the wheel when he was twenty-one years old. In 1959, Petty raced in the first Daytona 500, but his car broke down after twenty miles. Though his father won, the young Petty did well enough in that race and others to be named NASCAR Rookie of the Year. The following year, Petty won his first race, and from that point on, he was a solid, consistent driver.

Then, in 1964, things changed for Petty. Plymouth, which had been Petty's informal sponsor, decided to fully back his efforts. Before that, Plymouth's casual approach to auto racing meant that the Petty cars were sometimes up against higher-horsepower competition. Now, with Plymouth's full commitment, Petty was able to utilize the new Chrysler 426 hemispherical combustion chamber engine with high-end torque. That engine helped Petty establish dominance over the stock car racing world.

The difference that the new engine made in Petty's racing could be seen in the Daytona 500 that year. Petty won the event by setting a new world speed record of 154.3 miles per hour. That year, 1964, was also the year that Petty won his first NASCAR national championship. The very next year however, new NASCAR rules made Petty's engine illegal, and he left the sport to compete as a drag racer for a year.

Once he returned to NASCAR, there was no stopping "King Richard" and his famous chalk-blue No. 43 Plymouth. He became a major force in stock car racing, helping to push the sport to new heights of popularity. In 1966, he became the first driver to win two Daytona 500 contests, and the following year, he set a record by winning twenty-seven races. He won a third Daytona 500 in 1971, as well as the Dixie 500 that year, and earned more than $1 million in prize money. In 1979, he became the first owner-driver to win the Winston Cup.

Upon his retirement after the 1992 season, Petty had won the Daytona 500 seven times, was the NASCAR national driving champion seven times, and was the all-time NASCAR leader with 200 wins. When he retired, Petty formed Petty Enterprises, a complete stock car racing enterprise.

ROD LAVER is the only player to twice win the Grand Slam of tennis—Wimbledon plus the Australian, French, and U.S. Open championships—in a single year.

He was born in Rockhampton, Queensland, Australia in 1938. A sickly child, he seemed an unlikely candidate for future athletic stardom. However, even though he was small for a tennis player, he developed a devastating topspin ground stroke that befuddled opponents, and he became the Australian junior champion in 1957.

From 1959 to 1962, Laver was a member of the Australian Davis Cup team, which went undefeated during those years. In 1960, Laver won the men's singles title at the Australian championship, followed up in 1961 with a Wimbledon title in the men's singles category.

The next year, Laver won his first Grand Slam. He also won the Italian, Netherlands, Norwegian, and Swiss championships in 1962—an unprecedented feat demonstrating his total domination over the sport. It was little wonder that he was proclaimed the world's greatest tennis player that year.

Laver used a variety of shots to become a great tennis legend. He had a powerful volley stroke and a unique, spinning serve that was difficult to effectively return. His forehand and backhand were widely considered the best in tennis history.

Laver turned pro in 1963 and suffered a devastating beginning to his professional career, losing fourteen of his first sixteen matches. However, he maintained his game, and by 1965, he had turned things around completely.

As an amateur, Laver was rated number one in 1961 and 1962, and then, when he went pro, he was considered the world's top player from 1965 to 1967. (Pros weren't officially rated until 1968.) Subsequently, he was officially ranked number one as a pro in 1968 and 1969.

In 1968, Laver won Wimbledon for the third time and was the first pro to win the tournament. Then he had perhaps his greatest year ever in 1969 when he won seventeen singles titles and his second Grand Slam. Winning a second Grand Slam was unprecedented in tennis history.

Throughout his illustrious career, Laver won eight Grand Slam doubles championships and had forty-seven tournament victories. He won four times at Wimbledon, and brought home three Australian, two French, and two U.S. championship titles. Showing how completely dominant he was in the tennis world, Laver was rated a top-ten player until 1975 at the age of thirty-seven, in what traditionally has been a young person's sport.

JACK NICKLAUS has been called the greatest golfer of all time, and why not? No one who has ever picked up a golf club can compare with the **Golden Bear** in his prime, whom the PGA honored as Golfer of the Century in 1988.

Born in Columbus, Ohio, in 1940, Nicklaus inherited a love of sports from his athletic father. The young Nicklaus excelled in football, basketball, baseball, and track as well as golf, which he began playing at age ten. Six years later, he won his first tournament—the Ohio Open—and knew that golf was indeed his game.

Nicklaus concentrated on golf during his college years at Ohio State University in the late 1950s and early 1960s. In 1959, while playing on the U.S. Walker Cup team, he won two matches and played a significant role in the American team's victory. Unsure of his ability before that, he now understood his true potential.

In 1959, and again in 1961, Nicklaus won the U.S. Amateur Championships. However, it was in 1960 that Nicklaus began writing his own legend. That year he came in second to

the great **Arnold Palmer** in the U.S. Open. Nicklaus's 282 over 72 holes was the best score ever by an amateur. Between 1959 and 1961, he won all but one of the amateur tournaments he entered.

In November 1961, Nicklaus turned pro, and while he did not win any of the seventeen tournaments into which he entered, he always finished with money.

In 1962, he defeated Palmer in a playoff for the U.S. Open title, becoming the youngest player ever to win the tournament and beginning a heated rivalry between the two men.

Over the years, Nicklaus won six Masters Tournaments, five PGA championships, three more U.S. Open contests, three British Open titles, six Australian Open contests, and one World Open. A five-time PGA Player of the Year, his final Masters victory was in 1986 at the age of forty-six, making him the oldest champion in history. He was also a six-time Ryder Cup team member.

After he joined the senior tour in 1990, Nicklaus won the Senior Open tournament in 1991 and 1993. He has also won numerous athlete of the year awards and was *Sports Illustrated*'s Athlete of the Decade in 1980.

Over his career, Nicklaus has designed many golf courses, and in 1993, *Golf World* Magazine also named him Architect of the Year. Some of the courses he has designed routinely make Top 100 lists for golf courses in America.

As the winner of the Daytona 500, the Indianapolis 500, and the Formula One World Championship, **MARIO ANDRETTI** is one of the most successful and versatile race car drivers in history.

Mario and his twin brother Aldo were born in 1940 in Montona, a peaceful hillside village now known as Montovun, Croatia, having been ceded from Italy to Yugoslavia at the end of WWII. Despite this, Mario learned about auto racing and race cars at an early age. He went to see the *Mille Miglia* race as a boy and was completely hooked. With a motorcycle and a small coupe, he and his brother Aldo began racing.

The brothers didn't miss a beat when the Andretti family moved halfway across the globe to Nazareth, Pennsylvania, in 1955. They worked as mechanics and bought a modified 1948 Hudson to run on the stock car ovals. Initially, Aldo was the ace driver, but an accident at the track in Hatfield, Pennsylvania, forced him to the sidelines.

Mario moved behind the wheel, running modifieds, midgets, and three-quarter midgets, working as a mechanic by day and a driver by night. On Labor Day in 1963, he won three races at Hatfield and four at Flemington, New Jersey. Those seven same day victories convinced him that he was ready for the big time.

Even though his first USAC race in 1964 resulted in a spinout, his racing was impressive enough that he was offered a car to race by another racing team. It didn't take long for Andretti to prove that he truly belonged behind the wheel. In 1965, he became the USAC points champion and also had the fastest time for the first qualifying heats of the Indianapolis 500. Overall, he finished third in the race.

The following year, Andretti was again the USAC points champion. He also set a record by leading for 500 consecutive miles of championship racing, winning the Atlanta 300, Milwaukee 100, and the Langhorne 100. He began driving Championship GT cars, running a Ferrari to victory at Sebring. He also set a new lap record at Le Mans of 3:23.6.

In 1967, Andretti won the Daytona 500 in a Holman & Moody-prepared Ford Fairlaine. Two years later, he won the Indianapolis 500.

During the 1970s, it was Grand Prix Formula One racing that commanded the bulk of Andretti's attention. He won the Formula One championship in 1978 and then returned to Indy car racing.

Before he retired in 1994, Andretti had recorded four USAC/CART Championships, the 1965 Indy Rookie of the Year award, and second place on the all-time win list for Indy cars, with fifty-one victories. He also had the satisfaction of seeing his sons Michael and Jeff become excellent race car drivers.

◆ One of the most recognizable athletes in the entire world, **PELÉ** helped create a soccer boom in the United States with his athletic skills and charisma.

Pelé was born **Edson Arantes do Nascimento** in Três Corações, Brazil. His father was a soccer pro, but bad knees forced him to retire. His son inherited his love of the game, and Pelé and the neighborhood children played soccer from dawn to dusk, using a sock stuffed with newspapers that was wadded up into a ball. His father coached him, and Pelé and his friends played other local teams.

Soon, Pelé was playing on the junior squad of the Bauru city team. He led them to the junior championship three years in a row. He then signed with the Santos Football Club, a professional team, and scored a league record of 17 goals in his first year.

Chosen for the Brazilian World Cup team in 1958, he helped lead his country to the championship when they defeated Sweden 5–2. Pelé also led Brazil to the world title in 1962 and 1970, becoming the only player to be a member of three World Cup title teams.

Pelé's role in bringing championships to his team cannot be overestimated. Known for his powerful kicks and uncanny ball control, he was able to pass the ball to teammates at will, often without looking. Another facet of Pelé's game was his brilliant field strategy.

Pelé was an international hero whose presence once stopped a war between Biafra and Nigeria because both sides wanted to see him play. Pope **Paul VI** once said to him, "Don't be nervous, my son. I am more nervous than you, for I have been waiting to meet Pelé personally for a long time."

In 1970, Pelé scored his one-thousandth goal, making him the most prolific goal scorer in history. He retired from the Brazilian World Cup team in 1970, and then from Santos FC in 1974. However, **Clive Toye**, president of the New York City Cosmos of the North American Soccer League (NASL), begged him to play in America and "go down in history as the man who truly brought soccer to the United States."

Pelé played for the Cosmos from 1975 to 1977, leading them to a league championship in 1977. His contract with the Cosmos made him the highest paid athlete in the world, and he brought mystique and an unbelievable level of excitement to the games, helping to popularize soccer in America.

After his final retirement in 1977, Pelé became an international goodwill ambassador for the sport.

Two-time Olympic gold medal winner and eight-time world champion, **VASILY ALEXEYEV** was one of the greatest weightlifters in the history of the sport.

He was born in Russia in 1942. His father was a lumberjack, and by age twelve Alekseyev was already felling tree and lifting the logs for exercise. He worked in a timber/logging camp as a young man and impressed many with the ease with which he moved massive logs. He was already six feet by the time he was fourteen, and was wrestling on even terms with the full-grown woodsmen he worked with. It is said that his first barbell consisted of two wheels and an axle of a timber camp truck. Once, for breakfast, he was reported to have eaten twenty-six fried eggs and a steak.

Alexeyev first entered the world weightlifting scene on June 24, 1970. That day, he set three world records: the clean and jerk with 488.3 pounds, the press with 464.1 pounds, and the three-lift total with 1,311.7 pounds. Then, in September of that year, he jerked a weight over 500 pounds, breaking a weightlifting barrier as significant as the four-minute mile in track.

Two years later, at the 1972 Olympics, Alexeyev won the gold medal in the super heavyweight class. He set world records in all four categories of the weightlifting competition: the clean and jerk with 507.1 pounds, the press with 518.1 pounds, the snatch with 385.8 pounds, and the three-lift total with 1,411 pounds.

Four years later, at the 1976 Olympics, Alexeyev was again the story in the weightlifting competition. He broke his own record in the clean and jerk with a lift of 562.2 pounds, and his two-lift total—the press had been eliminated from in the competition—of 970 pounds gave him another gold medal.

Incredibly, Alexeyev stayed undefeated in the super heavyweight competition from 1970 through 1978, setting eighty world records from 1970–1977.

Unfortunately, Alexeyev was injured at the 1978 world championships, and his brilliant career went into decline. Nevertheless, before his retirement, Alexeyev accomplished weightlifting feats that no other athlete had ever attained before. He was inducted into the Weightlifting Hall of Fame in 1993.

The winner of twenty-four Grand Slam singles championships—more than any other woman—**MARGARET SMITH COURT** is one of the greatest players in the history of women's tennis.

She was born Margaret Jean Smith in Albury, New South Wales, Australia. Upon winning the 1960 Australian championships—later called the Australian Open—Smith became known for her rocket-like serve and volley. She went on to win that tournament ten more times, including a run of seven consecutive titles from 1960–1966.

In 1962, she won her first international tournament—the U.S. Singles championship (the present-day U.S. Open). The following year she became the first Australian woman to win at Wimbledon, which she won again in 1965. In 1966, Smith married **Barry Court**, had a child, and intended to retire. However, there was a lot of tennis left in her future.

Encouraged by her husband, who became her manager, she stepped back

out onto the court. Known from then on as Margaret Smith Court, she won the Australian, French, and U.S. Open titles in 1969. Then in 1970, she swept all four major titles—the Australian, French, and U.S. Opens, plus Wimbledon—becoming only the second woman at the time to win the Grand Slam in singles play. Her 46-game victory over **Billie Jean King** at Wimbledon was the longest women's single final in that tournament's history.

Smith Court had another child in 1972 but returned once more to competition the following year. She traveled with her husband, two children, and a nanny while rounding out another outstanding year, winning three of the four Grand Slam events—the Australian, French, and U.S. Open contests. She did lose a highly publicized match with 55-year-old **Bobby Riggs**, though, who was defeated later that year by Billie Jean King.

By 1973, she had won sixty-one major championships. That year, she was also the leading money-winner on the Virginia Slims circuit with winnings of $180,058.

During her career, she won twenty-four singles titles, nineteen women's doubles titles, and nineteen mixed doubles titles in Grand Slam tournaments. She also became the only player to win a Grand Slam in doubles and singles play. Her total of sixty-two Grand Slam titles is the most achieved by any woman.

A national hero in her home country of Australia, she was elected to the International Tennis Hall of Fame in 1979.

Rodeo cowboy is not a profession commonly thought of as producing great athletes, but in **LARRY E. MAHAN**, it might have produced the greatest rider of them all.

He was born on November 21, 1943, in Brooks, Oregon, and began riding in the rodeo at a children's competition in 1956. By 1962, Mahan had become the All-Around Oregon Cowboy champion and emerged triumphant in the bareback bronc riding and bulldogging events.

In 1963, Mahan joined the Rodeo Cowboys Association and began winning in his signature events of bareback bronc and saddle bronc riding. In the bull riding category, he won so often that he was the top money-winner in the event in 1965. He was the World Bull Riding Champion in 1965 and 1967.

In 1966, Mahan was the first cowboy to compete in three Rodeo Nationals final events. That year was also the beginning of his record five-year consecutive win streak for the All-Around Cowboy title.

Mahan earned so much in winnings that he was able to buy his own private plane that he used to travel to competitive events on the busy rodeo circuit. In 1967, he became the first rodeo star to earn more than $50,000 in a year. By 1971, he had earned over $280,000 throughout his career—another record. He became a media star as well, appearing on television and helping to popularize the rodeo cowboy lifestyle.

Mahan credited his successful career in rodeo to his love of horses. Horses are "my passion," he said. "Dad always had horses around. And it was horses that brought me into the rodeo."

In the early 1970s, Mahan suffered several injuries, sidelining him from professional competition much of the time, and yet he still continued to win events, including his sixth All-Around Cowboy title in 1973. After that win, he retired to a ranch he was able to purchase with his earnings.

In his later years, Mahan has spent much time at his rodeo schools for youngsters, and tends to various business interests. He also wrote a book, *Fundamentals of Rodeo Riding, a Mental and Physical Approach to Success*, and starred in a 1973 documentary movie, *The Great American Cowboy*, which won the 1973 Academy Award for Documentary Feature.

team to a thrilling 2–1 World Cup victory over Holland in the championship game in his home city of Munich.

Beckenbauer won the European Footballer of the Year Award twice in 1972 and 1976.

However, perhaps his most lasting contribution to the sport of soccer was to make a midcareer switch from midfielder to sweeper, and then turn that position into an offensive one. Traditionally, the sweeper had been purely a defensive position, but Beckenbauer's slashing style and aggressive play changed the sweeper into an offensive catalyst.

This radically changed the sport, creating a style of "total soccer," which meant that all players had to be ready to function in all capacities wherever they were on the field.

In 1977, Beckenbauer took his aggressive play across the ocean to America when he joined the New York Cosmos of NASL. Since he joined a team that already had Pelé (see no. 48), this meant that the Cosmos had the two best soccer players in the entire world.

Beckenbauer was voted the NASL Player of the Year in 1977. He helped lead the Cosmos to NASL championships in 1977, 1978, and 1980.

After retiring from play, Beckenbauer became the manager of the West German World Cup team in 1984. In 1990, he coached the team to a championship over Argentina, becoming the only person ever to have won the World Cup as both a player and a manager.

◆ One of soccer's great innovators, **FRANZ BECKENBAUER** originated an offensive use for the sweeper position, which revolutionized the tactics of the sport.

Beckenbauer was born on September 11, 1945 in Munich, in what would soon become postwar West Germany. Even in his youth, he showed a keen grasp of both the offensive and defensive sides of soccer, which would lead to his being recognized as a brilliant tactician and field general of the sport.

Beckenbauer joined the Bayern Munich team at the age of fourteen, and three years later, he gave up his job as a trainee insurance salesman to become a professional soccer player.

After struggling for a number of years, Beckenbauer's football club won the West German Cup in both 1966 and 1967. In 1971, Beckenbauer was made team captain, and beginning in 1974, he led Bayern Munich to three straight European titles. It was also in 1974 that he captained the West German

One of the great gymnasts in modern history, **KATŌ SAWAO** demonstrated his complete dominance over the sport by winning eight gold medals in three different Olympics.

Born in 1946 in Niigata Prefecture, Japan, Katō worked hard in his youth to win an Olympic gold. He was part of a nationwide movement that has made Japan a major force in Olympic gymnastics since 1960.

By the time of the 1968 Mexico City Olympics, Katō was ready to demonstrate his ability to the world. He went home a gold medalist in the individual all-around and floor exercise events, and bronze medalist in the rings. In addition, he was part of the Japanese team that won the gold in the all-around team competition.

Four years later, Katō again led the Japanese team to victory in the all-around team exercises at the 1972 Munich Olympics. Individually, he was the gold medalist in the all-around and parallel bars, and he also won silver medals in the pommel horse and the horizontal bars events.

In the 1976 Montreal Olympics, Katō shone once more. He won gold in the parallel bars and took home silver in the all-around category. In addition, he helped lead Japan to its fifth consecutive gold medal in the all-around team competition.

By that time, Katō had earned more gold medals than any other male gymnast in Olympic history. Plus his three silver and one bronze, his total of twelve medals ranks him high on the all-time list of Olympic medal winners. In 2001, Katō Sawao was inducted into the International Gymnastics Hall of Fame. He later became a professor at the same school he attended in Tokyo, University of Tsukaba, and became a coach. In 1994, his student Tanaka Hikaru won the Japanese national championship in gymnastics.

LAFFIT PINCAY JR. won the most races of anybody in horse racing history.

A native of Panama City, Panama, Pincay had horse racing in his genes as his father was also a jockey. When he was fifteen, Pincay made his first move to follow in his father's footsteps by getting a job at a track as a hot walker and by mucking out stalls. He worked for several hours a day and then went to school from the afternoon to the early evening. The young boy impressed people around the track with his horse-handling skills, and soon, he was riding horses out of the gate.

Pincay won his first race in 1964 on only his second career ride. Shortly thereafter, he came to the United States, where he won eight of his first eleven races. However, he spoke only Spanish and had to teach himself English by watching *Hollywood Squares* on television.

Pincay battled a lifelong weight problem, which probably contributed to a collapse he suffered in the jockey's room in 1974 at the Aqueduct Racetrack in New York. He reexamined his life, changed his diet, and emerged from his health crisis as a leaner, stronger, and healthier man.

Pincay was named winner of the Eclipse Award for outstanding jockey of the year five times in 1971, 1973, 1974, 1979, and 1985. It was the greatest number of times anybody has ever won the prestigious honor.

Pincay won the Belmont Stakes, one of horse racing's premier events, three years in a row from 1982–84. In 1984, he also won the Kentucky Derby. In 1985, he became the first jockey in history to earn over $13 million in a single year.

Pincay has won six Breeders' Cup races, which are run to determine thoroughbred racing's principal champions in different classes. However, the pinnacle of his career came in 1999, when he won his 8,834th race, eclipsing the legendary record victory total of **Bill Shoemaker** (see no. 37). The win also pushed his lifetime earnings to more than $270 million—another record.

Four years later, Pincay was still going strong. In January 2003, at the age of 56, he reached another career milestone, winning his 9,500th and 9,501st races at Santa Anita Park in California. However, in March, he was severely injured when another horse swung wide, knocked him off his mount, and rolled on him.

Pincay broke two bones in his neck during that accident, and while the breaks healed, his doctors advised him that his spine was not stable enough to ride again. In April, Pincay announced that he would retire from racing. His final victory total tallied up to 9,530.

Laffit Pincay Jr. was elected to horse racing's Hall of Fame in 1975.

◆ **KAREEM ABDUL-JABBAR**, pro basketball's all-time leading scorer, greatly changed the dynamics of the game's center position.

He was born **Ferdinand Lewis Alcindor Jr.**, in New York City in 1947, and first played basketball as a fourth-grade student. He was six feet, ten inches tall—and still growing—by the time he attended Powell Memorial High School. Like **Wilt Chamberlain** had done in high school, Alcindor dominated the sport. In his first year, Alcindor led the team to twenty-seven victories and the Catholic League championship. By the end of his senior year, Powell Memorial had won seventy-one games in a row and three straight league titles. During his high school career, Alcindor set a New York City record for total points scored with 2,067 and rebounds achieved with 2,002.

Attending college at the University of California at Los Angeles (UCLA), he led the school's basketball team to three straight NCAA championships. He was named MVP

of the NCAA tournament three times and was named College Player of the Year twice. It was also while he was at UCLA that he became a member of the Muslim faith and changed his name to Kareem Abdul-Jabbar.

The seven-foot, one-inch center turned pro in 1969, joining the Milwaukee Bucks of the NBA. In 1971, he led them to the NBA championship.

In 1975, Abdul-Jabbar was traded to the Los Angeles Lakers. He immediately turned that team into perennial NBA championship contenders. During the 1980s, along with such stars as **Magic Johnson** and **James Worthy**, Abdul-Jabbar led the Lakers to five championship titles.

Although he was very tall, Abdul-Jabbar was not a big and bulky man. Rather, he was almost too skinny to be an NBA center. However, he brought grace and fluidity to the position that had not been seen there before. With his unique "sky hook" shot that was nearly unstoppable, Abdul-Jabbar demonstrated that an NBA big man could do more than just intimidate opponents and grab rebounds. He could move around the court, get out of the paint to help his teammates on defense, and score from many different places.

Abdul-Jabbar was named the NBA's MVP six times during the regular season in 1971, 1972, 1974, 1976, 1977, and 1980 and twice during the playoffs in 1971 and 1985.

When he retired in 1989 after a stellar twenty-year career, Abdul-Jabbar was the all-time NBA leader in points scored, tallying an astonishing 38,387 points. He was also the leader in nineteen other categories, including blocked shots, field goal attempts, and field goal completions. He was voted into the Basketball Hall of Fame in 1994.

Winner of a gold medal in the 1972 Olympics, **DAN GABLE** was both a highly successful wrestler and a coach of the sport.

Born in Waterloo, Iowa, Gable did not lose a varsity wrestling match in high school. He continued this remarkable streak in college at Iowa State University until the final match of his senior year. Overall, his record in high school and college was 182–1.

Gable was a two-time NCAA champion in 1969 and 1970. In 1969, he was voted the NCAA tournament's Most Outstanding Wrestler.

For the next three years, Gable dedicated himself to one goal: training for the Olympics. He trained seven hours a day in preparation for the 1972 Games. Prior to that, Gable entered other competitions, and in 1971, he took home two gold medals—one from the Pan American Games and the other from the wrestling world championships.

The following year, all those long hours of dedicated training paid off. Despite a painful knee injury, Gable won the gold medal in the lightweight class at 149 pounds for freestyle wrestling at the Munich Olympics. He didn't give up a single point in his six matches.

Gable retired from wrestling in 1973 and joined the University of Iowa as the assistant coach of the wrestling team. In 1977, he became head coach. The team then ran off an unbelievable nine consecutive NCAA Intercollegiate Wrestling Championships victories from 1978–1986. After a five-year break, the team then won three more championships in a row from 1991–93.

Gable also coached American teams in several international freestyle competitions. He coached the 1984 U.S. Olympic team, which won seven gold medals. In 1985, he was inducted into the U.S. Olympic Hall of Fame.

Gable retired from coaching in 1998, having won a staggering fifteen NCAA championships in his twenty-one years as a head coach.

Before **BOBBY ORR** laced up his skates, hockey defensive players were supposed to do one thing and one thing only: play defense. However, Orr showed that defensive players could be offensive threats, too, and so he revolutionized the game of hockey.

Robert Gordon Orr was born in 1948, in Parry Sound, Ontario, Canada. He began playing street hockey at the tender age of four, and by the time he was in kindergarten, he was already in an organized league called the Parry Sound Minor Squirt Hockey League. Showing a glimpse of future greatness, he was named the league's MVP in the Pee Wee Division when he was nine years old.

Orr worked incessantly to perfect his hockey skills; he skated every day after school until the sun set and only darkness could put a halt to his playing. All of Orr's hard work paid off, too. When he was just fourteen, he was signed to an amateur contract with the Boston Bruins of the NHL.

Orr had an outstanding career in junior hockey and came up to the Bruins for the 1966–1967 season. He won the Calder Trophy as NHL's outstanding rookie for that season.

It didn't take him long to totally redefine the role of a defender in hockey. Prior to Orr, defensive players had been content to remain by the goalie and assist when the other team went on the attack. Orr showed that players on defense could play offensively. He was a lightning-fast skater, and he thrilled fans with his headlong rushes up the ice, charging toward the other team's goalie with the puck in his possession.

In fact, Orr won the NHL's scoring title in both 1970 and 1975—a feat usually accomplished by traditionally high scorers like wings or centers. He was the first defensive player to win the scoring crown.

Although he only played nine seasons due to knee problems, Orr piled up numerous individual honors. In 1969 and 1970, he was named NHL's MVP. He also won the Norris Trophy, which is awarded to the league's best defensive player, for eight straight seasons. Orr was also a first team All-Star for eight consecutive seasons.

The Bruins won two Stanley Cups during Orr's tenure with them in 1970 and 1972. Both years, he personally won the Conn Smythe Trophy for his outstanding performance in the playoffs.

Orr played his final few seasons with the Chicago Blackhawks, but by then, knee injuries had reduced him to a shadow of his former self. He retired in 1979 and was elected to the NHL Hall of Fame the same year.

In the long history of the Olympic Games, no athlete had ever won seven gold medals in its long history, no athlete had ever won seven gold medals in a single Olympic Games until American swimmer **MARK SPITZ** accomplished the feat in 1972.

A native of Modesto, California, it wasn't until his family moved to Sacramento when he was eight years old that Spitz began swimming competitively. He trained at the Santa Clara Swim Club as a teenager. In 1967, he set world records in the 400-meter freestyle as well as in the 100- and 200-meter butterfly.

In 1968, Spitz created somewhat of a controversy by announcing that he would win six medals at that year's Olympics. He fell short of his ambitious goal, however, winning just two gold medals as a member of the 4 × 100-meter and 4 × 200-meter freestyle relay teams. He also won a silver and bronze, respectively, in the 100-meter

butterfly and 100-meter freestyle events. Still, it was a disappointing performance for an athlete who was determined to dominate his sport. It would be another four years before that happened.

After the 1968 Olympics, Spitz entered Indiana State University. Over the next four years, he won numerous NCAA and AAU titles in the 100-, 200-, and 500-yard butterfly and freestyle events. As captain of the school's swim team, he helped continue its run of six consecutive NCAA championships from 1968–1973. In 1971, Spitz won the Sullivan Award as the top amateur athlete in the United States.

Then came the 1972 Munich Olympics, and Mark Spitz's historic hour. He set world records and took home the gold in all four individual events that he entered. In the 100-meter freestyle, his time was a record 51.2 seconds. In the 200-meter freestyle, he set another record with a time of 1:52.78. He won the 100-meter butterfly competition in a record 54.27 seconds and set a fourth record in winning the 200-meter butterfly in 2:00.07.

Spitz also won three more gold medals as a member of the U.S. team, which won the 400-meter freestyle relay, the 800-meter freestyle relay, and the 400-meter medley relay. The U.S. team victories in these events also set new world record times.

After his phenomenal success at the Olympics, Spitz retired from swimming. He was greatly in demand for a time as a media personality and a spokesperson for television commercials. Twenty years after his triumphs, he attempted a comeback for the 1992 Olympics, but age had robbed him of his skills, and he failed to qualify for the Games.

In 1983, Mark Spitz became one of the first inductees into the U.S. Olympic Hall of Fame.

◆ **GUSTAV THÖNI** is one of the greatest alpine skiers in all history.

He was born on February 28, 1951, and as a young man, he became so proficient at skiing that he was recognized as a leader of the so-called "new breed" of Italian alpine skiers.

Like other members of this new breed, Thöni's specialties were the slalom and the giant slalom, events that demand speed, agility, and a fierce competitive spirit. While the downhill race is a contest of sheer speed and cornering over a vertical course, the slalom emphasizes technical virtuosity.

The race runs over a switchback-style course, with demanding and quick, short turns that wind through various combinations of gates.

In the slalom men's competition, there are fifty-five to seventy-five gates, and the length of the course is comparatively short, at 459–722 feet, while for women, there are forty to sixty gates on a course ranging from 394–722 feet.

In the giant slalom, the gates are fewer and farther apart, and the race is run on a longer course, from 820–1,312 feet for men, and 820–984 feet for women. Each skier races twice, and the total of both runs determines the winner.

In 1970, before he was even twenty years old, Thöni was the leader in the World Cup giant slalom standings. The following year, he won his first overall World Cup title—the first of four that he would capture. He was the first Italian skier to be an overall World Cup champion.

Thöni had perhaps his greatest year in 1972. He won the overall World Cup title again and was again the leader in the giant slalom rankings. However, his biggest triumph that year came at the Winter Olympic Games in Sapporo, Japan. He won a gold

medal in the giant slalom, and a silver medal in the slalom.

The following year, Thöni won his third consecutive overall World Cup title. After missing out on the overall title in 1974, Thöni again captured the crown in 1975, concluding a remarkable streak of four World Cup titles in five years. Thöni was again prominent at the next Olympics in 1976, winning his second silver medal in the slalom at Innsbruck, Austria.

In addition to his World Cup victories, Thöni won two Fédération internationale de ski (FIS) World Alpine Ski Championships held on the legendary ski slopes of St. Moritz in 1974 for the slalom and giant slalom.

After his retirement from competitive skiing in the late 1970s, Thöni became a coach. He had the pleasure of seeing one of his trainees, the great **Alberto Tomba**, also become a champion international skier.

One of the greatest athletes ever to emerge from the Soviet Union, **NIKOLAI ANDRIANOV** is also one of the few athletes in Olympic history to win seven gold medals.

Born on October 14, 1952, Andrianov showed so much gymnastic aptitude as a child that he was placed into the Soviet system for that sport at an early age. (At that time in the Soviet Union, any young child who demonstrated skill in any athletic endeavor was intensively directed toward that sport.)

By the time of the 1972 Olympic Games in Munich, Germany, Andrianov was ready to demonstrate his astounding ability to the world. He won a gold medal in the floor exercise with a score of 19.175 points, beating out two strong Japanese competitors, **Akinori Nakayama** and **Shigeru Kasamatsu**, who won silver and bronze, respectively. Adrianov also won a bronze medal in the long horse vault event that year.

By 1976, the Soviet men's gymnastics team, as well as teams from other Eastern European countries, were poised to break the dominance of the Japanese men's team. As one of the leaders of the Soviet team, Andrianov led the charge.

In the Montreal Games that year, Andrianov won the gold medal in the all-around competition with 116.65 points, beating two-time defending Olympic champion and great Japanese gymnast **Katō Sawao** (see no. 53). The Soviet challenger also won three other gold medals in the long horse vault with 19.45 points, the rings with 19.65 points, and the floor exercise with 19.45 points.

Rounding out his collection of medals and winning performances that year, Andrianov won silver in the parallel bars and bronze in the pommel horse. Although Japan won gold in the team combined exercises for the fifth straight Olympics, Andrianov had helped ramp up the Soviet team as a rising powerhouse in gymnastics.

In 1980, it all came together for the Soviet team at the Olympics they hosted in Moscow. The Soviets won gold in the team combined event, and Andrianov took home gold in the long horse vault competition. In addition, **Aleksandr Dityatin** won gold medals for the all-around competition and the rings, and **Aleksandr Tkachyov** took the gold in the parallel bars.

With his participation in three Olympics, Adrianov holds the career record for the most medals won with fifteen, as well as being in the elite group of athletes who have won seven gold medals.

One of the top global tennis players in the 1970s and 1980s, **JIMMY CONNORS** led a new wave of feisty and aggressive play that dominated the sport's professional ranks.

Connors was born in Belleville, Illinois, in 1952. One apocryphal story about his childhood holds that, by his third birthday, his mother Gloria had put a tennis racket in his hands and had him practicing. What is known to be true is that his mother was a professional tennis instructor who taught him the game. She also instilled in him the aggressiveness that marked his playing career.

When Connors was a teenager, his family moved to California so he could receive expert training and coaching from tennis greats **Pancho Gonzales** and **Pancho Segura**. While attending college at UCLA, Connors won the NCAA men's singles title in 1971. After turning pro in 1972, Connors won his first two tournaments.

However, his breakout year professionally came in 1974. He won three of four Grand Slam tournaments that year—the Australian Open, Wimbledon, and the U.S. Open. He was banned from playing in the French Open, the fourth Grand Slam tournament, because of a prior contract he had signed to play in the professional World TeamTennis league.

Connors was the leader of a new type of tennis player that was highly volatile, critical, and even verbally abusive toward linesmen—and arguing continually over lost points. His behavior was the complete opposite of the quiet prototype of the traditional tennis player. Among those who played tennis in this aggressive manner were the sharp-tempered Romanian **Ilie Nastase** and American **John McEnroe**.

Connors matched his personality and behavior with an aggressive style of tennis. A left-hander who used a two-handed backhand, Connors was known for his relentless manner on the court. An opponent once said of him, "Playing him is like fighting Joe Frazier. The guy's always coming at you. He never lets up."

Connors won five U.S. Open titles and two Wimbledon championships during his career. He also set all-time records by winning eighty-four Wimbledon matches and ninety-eight U.S. Open matches. His 109 career wins in professional singles championship matches is another record.

As he aged, the once-abrasive Connors mellowed, behaving more graciously on and off the court and winning over many tennis fans who had once disliked him. He was among the top ten in rankings until 1988. He then retired, but made a strong comeback in 1991, beating much younger opponents and making it all the way to the semifinals of the U.S. Open.

In 1993, Connors helped found a seniors tour for players over thirty-five years old. He was inducted into the Tennis Hall of Fame in 1998.

ANNEMARIE MOSER-PRÖLL won six World Cup titles during the 1970s—more than any other skier at the time—and she had never taken a single skiing lesson in her life.

As a child in Kleinarl, Salzburg, Austria, Moser-Pröll grew up in the Alps. She made her own skis when she was four years old and began teaching herself to ski. However, unlike many others who excel in a particular sport and go on to study with a teacher, Moser-Pröll never had a professional lesson. Instead, she developed her own techniques and mastery of the slopes.

She learned quickly and well. When she was fifteen years old, she became a member of the Austrian national ski team. Although she was superb in all three racing events—the downhill, the giant slalom, and the slalom—it was the downhill on which she focused her energy.

Moser-Pröll was the youngest skier to ever win the World Cup overall championship, which she achieved during the 1970–1971 season. She then won this title four more years in a row, and a sixth time later that same decade. She also won the World Cup giant slalom three times in 1971, 1972, and 1975. Demonstrating her dominance in the downhill, she won the Women's World Cup downhill championship seven times—an all-time record.

Moser-Pröll did not ignore the Olympics either. At the 1972 Games in Sapporo, Japan, she won silver medals in the giant slalom and downhill events.

She got married between the 1973 and 1974 seasons, but that did not slow her down. She continued to ski competitively—and win. She set an all-time mark by recording thirty-three wins in World Cup downhill events. She also finished second in lifetime wins in the World Cup giant slalom and World Cup combined events.

Moser-Pröll retired at the conclusion of the 1974–1975 skiing season. However, she returned to the competitive arena in 1978 and won her sixth World Cup title. Capping off a brilliant career, she won a gold medal in the downhill event at the 1980 Winter Olympics.

RAISA SMETANINA had an Olympic career of incredible success and longevity. In a competition that is usually reserved for the youngest and the strongest, the Soviet skier won ten medals over five Olympics in just twenty years.

Smetanina began her remarkable "medal run" at the 1976 Olympics at Innsbruck, Austria. She won gold in the women's 10K cross-country skiing event, and a silver in the 5K cross-country competition. Both were tight contests with **Helena Takalo** of Finland. That year, Smetanina won another gold as part of the first-place Soviet women's 20K relay team.

In the 1980 Games held in Lake Placid, New York, she picked right up where she left off. She won gold in the women's 5K cross-country race, defeating **Hikka Riihivuori** of Finland, who won silver. Smetanina also won a silver medal as a member of the Soviet women's 20K relay team.

Four years later, Smetanina won two silver medals at the Olympics in Sarajevo—one in the women's 10K cross-country race, and another in the women's 20K cross-country event. In both events, she was beaten for the gold by **Marja-Liisa Hamalainen** of Finland.

In the 1988 Games in Calgary, Canada, Smetanina won two more medals: a silver in the 10K, and a bronze in the 20K. She then picked up her record tenth medal at the 1992 Games in Albertville, France, winning a gold as part of the women's 20K relay team playing under a banner called "The Unified Team," made up of athletes from the former Soviet Union.

After Smetanina won her tenth medal, she retired, having set a record in Nordic skiing that will be hard to match.

A gentle and friendly man everywhere else, **WALTER PAYTON** was a terror on the field and known as perhaps the greatest all-around running back in the history of the NFL.

Payton was born in Columbia, Mississippi. He attended college at Jackson State University, where he set a college football record for points scored. When he graduated in 1975, the NFL's Chicago Bears drafted him, leading him to set another record. His was the highest paying contract ever given to a rookie.

Payton quickly proved that he was worth it. After rushing for 679 yards in his first year, he ran for at least 1,200 yards in ten out of the next eleven seasons. Beginning in 1976, he led the league's National Football Conference in rushing for the first of five straight years and was named to the Pro Bowl for the first of nine times. The following year, he ran for a career-high 1,852 yards and scored 14 touchdowns, helping the Bears make the playoffs for the first time in fourteen years.

In 1977, Payton ran for a then-record 275 yards in a single game and finished the year with an average yards per carry of 5.5. He was voted the NFL's MVP that year, the first of two times he would receive that honor.

Payton was the league's MVP once again in the 1985 season, when he ran for more than 1,500 yards. The Bears were the best team in football that year, posting a record of 15–1 and winning the 1986 Super Bowl.

Despite the tremendous physical punishment that NFL running backs receive, Payton only missed one game during his thirteen-year career. He credited that to a rigorous off-season training regimen that included running up steep hills near his home. That undoubtedly contributed to his incredible leg strength. Time and again on the field, Payton would seem trapped by a defender, only to stick out a leg and then yank it free from the grasp of a tackler. In contrast to his toughness, Payton had a gentle disposition and was nicknamed **"Sweetness"** by his teammates.

Payton retired after the 1987 season. At that time, he was the NFL's leading rusher, with 16,726 yards. (That record was broken by **Emmitt Smith** of the Dallas Cowboys in 2002.) During his career, Payton also had 492 pass receptions for 4,538 yards, bringing his combined yardage total to 21,264. He also scored 125 touchdowns—110 of them rushing.

In 1993, Payton was inducted into the Pro Football Hall of Fame. He died in 1999 of a rare liver disease.

One of the most successful and popular women's tennis players in history, **CHRIS EVERT** won eighteen Grand Slam singles championships, ranking third on the all-time list.

She was born in Fort Lauderdale, Florida, and grew up in a family in which tennis was a passion. Her parents and four siblings were all dedicated players. The kids won competitions, and their father was the coach.

Evert got her first racket when she was five and developed a dedicated practice routine as a child. She entered every age group competition available, so that by the time she was twelve years old, she was ranked number two in the United States for that age group. At age sixteen, she was ranked number one nationally, and she won forty-six straight matches that year. Then she debuted at the U.S. Open in Forest Hills and made it all the way to the semifinals, becoming the youngest woman in history

to do so. At age seventeen, she won the $100,000 Virginia Slims Tournament at Boca Raton—the most lucrative women's tournament at the time.

Evert turned pro in 1973 and won six of seven tournaments she entered. She won fifteen tournaments in her second pro year, including Wimbledon, the Canadian Open, and the French Open. In 1974, she was the Associated Press's Woman Athlete of the Year. The following year, she was ranked number one, and won her first U.S. Open title.

Evert was at her best in Grand Slam events. She won the U.S. Open four years in row from 1975–78, and then again in 1980 and 1982. She was a finalist at the French Open ten years in a row, spanning 1973–1982, and won the title seven times. With her three Wimbledon crowns and two Australian Open titles, she had a total of eighteen Grand Slam singles championships, which ranks her third behind **Margaret Smith Court** (see no. 50) and **Helen Wills Moody** (see no. 20.)

One of the first players to use a two-handed backhand, Evert was never flashy. She was steady and consistent as a player, and she earned the nickname **Little Miss Icicle** for her nearly unflappable demeanor during matches.

Evert also made some headlines during her romance with fellow American tennis star **Jimmy Connors** in the 1970s. She married British tennis star **John Lloyd** in 1979, but they divorced in 1987. After that, she married former American Olympic skier **Andy Mill** in 1988.

Evert retired in 1990, while still near the top of her game. In 1995, she was unanimously voted into the International Tennis Hall of Fame.

One of the greatest cyclists of all time, **BERNARD HINAULT** won the Tour de France five times.

Hinault was born in 1954 on the northern coast of Brittany, France. As a young boy, he rode his bike at least fifteen miles every day. After four years of training as a runner, he watched his cousin win a bicycle race in 1971 and decided that he wanted to try racing as well. Borrowing his brother's bike, he rode it to victory in his first race. From then on, he was hooked and went on to win twelve of the twenty events he entered in 1971. The following year, he won the French national junior championship.

Following a stint in the military that did not afford him any bike-riding opportunities, Hinault returned to the sport and quickly became one of its dominant athletes. In 1974, he won thirteen races including the national pursuit championship.

Turning pro that same year, Hinault became known as **"The Badger"** because of his cool, calculating racing personality and aggressive riding style. During the 1970s and 1980s, he won almost every European cycling event, including the Vuelta a España (Tour of Spain) in 1978 and 1983; the Giro d'Italia (Tour of Italy) in 1980, 1982, and 1985; and the world championship road race.

Hinault went out for the Tour de France fully prepared. He first won the event in 1978, with a time of 108 hours and 18 minutes. The following year, he won it again. The race totaled 2,200 miles and took nearly a month to complete. Hinault won it with a time of 103:06.50.

In 1980, however, he had to drop out of the race with tendinitis, but in 1981, he was healthy again and won the race for a third time, with a time of 96:19.38.

Typical of Hinault's riding personality was his victory in the 1982 Tour de France.

The distance was 2,181 miles, with the cyclists covering it in increments of about 100 miles. Hinault staged a dramatic, come-from-behind charge in the last stage of the race to overtake the leader and win the event for the fourth time. His fifth victory came in 1985.

Hinault's outspoken and confident manner made him a hero throughout France and elevated the sport of cycling to new heights of popularity. When he retired in 1986, Hinault had 194 professional victories to his credit.

That year, he was voted Top French Athlete of the Last 60 Years.

LARRY BIRD not only helped revitalize a historic pro basketball franchise that had fallen on hard times, but he injected new life into the entire NBA.

Bird was born in the Indiana town of French Lick, and after starring on his high school team, he attended Indiana State University on a scholarship. In his senior year in 1979, Bird was named the College Player of the Year as he led the team to an undefeated regular season and took them all the way to the NCAA championship game, where they lost to a Michigan State team led by **Magic Johnson** (see no. 73).

Bird was drafted as a forward by the once-mighty Boston Celtics, who had fallen on hard times in the late seventies. He had an immediate impact on the Celtics, reviving the team to a first-place finish in their division in 1980. He was named NBA's Rookie of the Year that season.

The following year, Bird led the Celtics to the NBA championship. Boston won two more titles during Bird's career in 1984 and 1986, and both times, he was voted MVP in the playoffs. Bird was also named the league's MVP for three straight years from 1984–1986.

In the 1986–1987 season, Bird became the first player in basketball history to shoot at least .500 from the floor and at least .900 from the free throw line. One of the best shooting forwards in NBA history, he was also a superb passer, often getting the ball to a teammate without looking in his direction.

Along with Magic Johnson of the Los Angeles Lakers, Bird was credited with renewing fan interest in the NBA. It was no secret that the league had been struggling before his arrival. Ticket sales were down, there were no real marquee players, and fan interest was waning. However, Bird changed all that with his dynamic play.

He and Johnson maintained a spirited but friendly rivalry throughout the 1980s as they dueled on the court, and their teams battled for the league championship on several occasions.

A bad back hastened Bird's retirement before the 1992–1993 season just after he had won a gold medal as a member of the U.S. Olympic Basketball Team. He left the game with lifetime totals of 21,791 points (a 24.3 average per game), 8,974 rebounds, and an .886 free throw shooting percentage.

After his retirement, Bird became the coach of NBA's Indiana Pacers. He led the team to the playoffs several times but could not get into the championship round. In 1998, he was elected to the Basketball Hall of Fame.

RAY CHARLES LEONARD was one of the greatest boxers of his era and the first prizefighter to win titles in five different weight classes.

Born in Wilmington, North Carolina, he was named Ray Charles by his mother, who wanted him to be a singer. Instead, after he became a successful prizefighter, he got the nickname **"Sugar Ray"** after **Sugar Ray Robinson**, the famous boxer of the 1940s and 1950s.

As an amateur, Leonard compiled an amazing record of 145–5 with seventy-five knockouts. He won the National Golden Gloves, two international championships, and two gold medals as a light welterweight—one at the 1975 Pan American Games and another at the 1976 Montreal Olympics.

Leonard's plan was to retire from boxing after the Olympics, but family financial needs changed his thinking. As a result, he turned pro in 1977. Two years later, he defeated **Wilfredo Benitez** to win the World Boxing Council (WBC) welterweight crown,

only to lose it to **Roberto Duran** in 1980. The rematch held later that year was one of the most famous boxing matches in history. Duran, who had a reputation as a tough guy, suddenly lowered his hands during the eighth round, cried out "¡No más!" in Spanish (meaning, "No more!"), and walked back to his corner, though seemingly unhurt.

In 1981, Leonard won the World Boxing Association (WBA) welterweight title from Tommy **"Hit Man"** Hearns, as well as the WBA junior middleweight championship by knocking out **Ayub Kalue**.

Leonard was a champion for the ages—a fighter who had the punching power of a mule kick, and the speed and agility of a ballet dancer. In addition, he was an extremely intelligent and photogenic man, which made him perfect for television. This combination of ability and good looks propelled him to great popularity.

It seemed as if he would dominate his weight classes for a long time, but in 1982, he suffered from the rare condition of a detached retina, which forced him into early retirement.

Leonard returned to the ring for one more fight in 1984, and then retired again. However, he returned yet again in 1987, moving up in weight class, and winning the WBC middleweight title from **Marvin Hagler**. The next year, he won the WBC light heavyweight and super middleweight titles, making him the first boxer to win titles in five different weight classes.

However, Leonard was not quite the same devastating fighter he had been before his eye injury. After losing a bout in 1991, he didn't fight again for six years. In 1997, he returned to the ring but lost and then quit boxing for good. In 1997, he was inducted into the International Boxing Hall of Fame.

JOE MONTANA, at the peak of his career, was one of the greatest quarterbacks in the history of the NFL, leading the San Francisco 49ers to four Super Bowl titles.

A native of Monongahela, Pennsylvania, Montana went to college at the University of Notre Dame. There, he quickly gained a national reputation as a pinpoint passer and outstanding field general. He won acclaim especially for his ability to bring his team up from behind—the most famous example of this being the 1979 Cotton Bowl, in which he rallied Notre Dame from a 23-point deficit in the fourth quarter to defeat the University of Houston, 35–34.

Drafted by the NFL's San Francisco 49ers in 1979, Montana quickly lifted that team from the depths of obscurity to rise as one of the most dominant in league history. Montana became the starting quarterback in his second season and led the league with a 64.5 completion percentage. The next season, he quarterbacked the 49ers

into the playoffs and then led them to a 26–21 victory over the Cincinnati Bengals in the 1982 Super Bowl. In that game, he was fourteen for twenty-two in passing for 157 yards and one touchdown. He also scored another touchdown rushing and was voted the game's MVP.

In 1985, Montana got the team to the Super Bowl again, where they defeated the Miami Dolphins, 38–16. Once more, Montana was brilliant, completing twenty-four of thirty-five passes for 331 yards and two touchdowns. He was, again, voted the game's MVP.

With Montana at the helm, the 49ers won the Super Bowl twice more in 1989 and 1990. In the 1989 game, in a rematch against the Bengals, Montana engineered one of his famous "comeback" drives that took the 49ers ninety-two yards in the game's final two minutes to squeak out a 20–16 victory. In 1990, Montana simply took apart a good Denver Broncos squad. He completed twenty-two passes in twenty-nine attempts for 297 yards and five touchdowns as the 49ers cruised to victory, 55–10. Montana was once again the game's MVP, becoming the first three-time winner of the award.

Montana played his final two seasons with the Kansas City Chiefs but could not repeat his magic with them. Sadly, the team never made it to the Super Bowl.

Montana retired after the 1994 season. For his career, he had an incredible 93.5 quarterback rating, was third in career completions with 2,929, fifth in career passing yardage with 35,124, and sixth in career touchdown passes with 244. He led the NFL in passing five times and was named to the Pro Bowl eight times.

In 2000, he was inducted into the Pro Football Hall of Fame.

No discussion of great tennis players can leave out **MARTINA NAVRATILOVA**, who is one of the best players ever to pick up a racket.

Born in Prague, Czechoslovakia (present-day Czech Republic), her parents had an unhappy marriage and divorced when Martina was three. Her father died tragically six years later. Her mother loved to play tennis and often took Martina to the courts with her. In 1961, her mother married **Mike Navratil**, and Martina's name became Navratilova when she added the Czech suffix for "daughter of." Navratil taught his stepdaughter to play tennis, and when he took her to see **Rod Laver** play in a tournament, she decided then and there that she wanted to become a tennis player.

At the age of eight, Navratilova competed in her first tournament and made the semifinals. The next year, she began practicing under the watchful eye of **George Parma**, the great Czech tennis coach.

By the time she was fourteen years old, Navratilova had won the National Championship for her age group. Three years later, she was her country's number one woman player, with three National Women's Championships and the National Junior Championships to her credit.

However, Navratilova was growing increasingly frustrated by the Czechoslovakian Tennis Federation's interference with her career. Finally in 1975, while playing in the U.S. Open, she asked for political asylum and defected to America.

After this point, her brilliant career kicked into high gear. In 1975, she and partner **Chris Evert** (see no. 65) won the French Open doubles championship, and then the following year, they swept the Wimbledon doubles championship.

By the late 1970s, Navratilova began to dominate Wimbledon in singles play. She won the tournament in 1978 and 1979, and then six years in a row from 1982–1987. In 1990, she won it again, giving her an amazing nine Wimbledon titles.

Navratilova held the top rank in the world for all but twenty-two weeks of a five-year, 282-week period from 1982–1987. During the 1980s, she won four U.S. Open contests, three Australian Open contests, and two French Open contests.

Navratilova proved to be just as good at doubles tennis as she was at singles. She won thirty-one women's doubles titles in Grand Slam events, many of which were played with **Pam Shriver**. Although she retired from singles competition in the early 1990s, Navratilova was still going strong in doubles in 2003. At the age of forty-six, she won the Australian Open mixed doubles championship, becoming the oldest person to win a Grand Slam event. It was her fifty-seventh Grand Slam title, second all-time to the sixty-two won by **Margaret Smith Court** (see no. 50).

ERIC HEIDEN was a unique athlete and individual who accomplished the unprecedented feat of winning five individual gold medals in the Olympics. Then, after the victories, he walked away from his sport, turning his back on fame and potential for huge financial gain.

A native of Madison, Wisconsin, Heiden began skating at the age of two. As he grew older, he added running, cycling, and weightlifting to his training regimen. When he was a teenager, Heiden began training as a speed skater with his sister Beth, who would also go on to participate in the Olympics.

In 1976, Heiden was on the cusp of greatness. That same year, he participated in the Olympic Games at Innsbruck, Austria, but he did not win a medal. He also finished fifth in the world speed skating championships.

That proved to be Heiden's "warm-up" year. In 1977, at the age of 18, Heiden won the world junior overall, senior overall, and sprint speed skating championships—an unprecedented sweep. His victory was the first ever by an American in the event.

Heiden continued his dominance of the world championships over the next three years. He swept all three championships in 1978 and won both the sprint and overall titles again in 1979 and 1980. Along the way, he set new world records in the 10,000-meter race in 1979 and the 1,000- and 1,500-meter races in 1980.

However, Heiden's biggest triumphs were witnessed at the 1980 Winter Olympic Games in Lake Placid, New York. He won an incredible five gold medals for his individual performance in speed skating events. It was the only time in Olympic history that anyone has ever won five gold medals for individual events. In the process, Heiden set two world records and three Olympic records.

Heiden simply dominated every speed skating event from the sprints to the endurance races. His victories and record-setting times were: 500 meters in 38.03 seconds; 1,000 meters in 1:15.18; 1,500 meters in 1:55.44; 5,000 meters in 7:02.29; and 10,000 meters in 14.28.13. His victories in the 500- and 10,000-meter races set world record times, while he also broke Olympic records in the other three events.

For his landmark performance, Heiden received the Sullivan Award as the top American amateur athlete of 1980. After the Olympics, Heiden announced his retirement, and although commercial endorsements were showered upon him, he refused them all.

Heiden later became a competitive cyclist, but his moment in the spotlight ended after the 1980 Olympics. He summed up his view on fame and stardom right after his retirement when he said, "I really liked it best when I was a nobody."

With her athletic ability, exuberant attitude, and wild-colored attire, **FLORENCE GRIFFITH JOYNER** captured the hearts of a generation. Only her untimely death prevented her from reaching greater heights of popularity.

Born in Los Angeles, Florence began running track at age seven and won the Jesse Owens National Youth Games at fourteen years old. She set records in sprinting and the long jump at Jordan High School, and then enrolled at California State University to train under famed track coach **Bob Kersee**.

When Kersee moved to UCLA, so did Florence. She was the National Collegiate Athletic Association's 200-meter race champion in 1982 and then won the NCAA 400-meter event in 1983. After winning a silver medal at the 1984 Olympics in the 200-meter dash, she went into semiretirement.

In 1987 she married **Al Joyner**, an Olympic gold medalist and the brother of track star **Jackie Joyner-Kersee**, who was the wife of Griffith's coach. That year, Griffith also re-emerged in the track-and-field spotlight by winning the 200-meter dash at the world championship games in Rome and finishing second overall in the competition.

However, 1988 was to be the year of "FloJo," as she came to be known. In the Olympic trials on July 16, she set a 100-meter dash record of 10.49—a full quarter-second off the previous mark. No one in history had beaten the existing 100-meter dash time record by more than one-tenth of a second up to that point. The following day, she set a U.S. record for the 200-meter run at 21.77 seconds.

Primed and ready for the Olympics, FloJo won three gold medals in the Games in Seoul, Korea. She won the individual 100- and 200-meter dashes and was a member of the winning 400-meter relay team. She also won a silver medal in the 1,600-meter relay.

With her Olympic triumphs came a host of awards. She was named Sportswoman of the Year in France and Athlete of the Year by the Soviet news agency Telegrafnoye Agentstvo Sovetskogo Soyuza (TASS). In 1989, she won the U.S. Olympic Committee Award, Berlin's Golden Camera Award, the Sullivan Award as the top American amateur athlete, and the Jesse Owens Award as the outstanding track-and-field athlete of the year.

FloJo's one-legged running suits, designer running shoes, and long, multicolored fingernails made her a sensation with the media and young sports fans; soon she had a number of lucrative business enterprises going, including fashion design, writing, and acting.

In 1989, she announced her retirement from track to tend to her outside interests. In September 1998, she died of suffocation in her sleep after suffering an epileptic fit. She was just thirty-eight years old.

The engaging smile and upbeat personality of **EARVIN "MAGIC" JOHNSON JR.** masked a fierce competitive spirit and a drive to win that helped the Los Angeles Lakers garner five NBA championships in the 1980s.

Johnson acquired the nickname "Magic" after a magnificent high school game in his hometown of Lansing, Michigan, in which he scored 36 points, had 18 rebounds, and dished out 16 assists. Playing point guard as a sophomore for Michigan State University, Johnson led the school in a victorious effort against **Larry Bird's** Indiana State University for the 1979 NCAA championship. The Bird-Johnson rivalry would continue throughout the 1980s as both players moved into the professional ranks.

Leaving college after that year, Johnson joined the Los Angeles Lakers of the NBA. His play-making ability combined with his high-grade enthusiasm were the magic ingredients the Lakers needed to reach championship heights. Along with **Kareem Abdul-Jabbar**, Johnson sparked the Lakers immediately that season and they won the 1980 championship. With Johnson running the Lakers' high-powered "Showtime" offense, the team won four more NBA titles in the 1980s in 1982, 1985, 1987, and 1988.

Johnson was considered one of the greatest point guards and playmakers in NBA history, piling up numerous individual honors. In 1980, he was the first rookie to be named MVP of the NBA championship finals. He was the league championship series MVP twice more in 1982 and 1987 and was NBA's MVP three times in 1987, 1989, and 1990.

Along with the Boston Celtics' Larry Bird, Johnson is credited with revitalizing public interest in the NBA. The Bird-Johnson, Celtics-Lakers duels on the court were exciting to watch. In particular, Johnson's charismatic smile and enthusiastic personality were always in demand with television networks, which helped the NBA gain even more exposure.

Johnson stunned the sports world in late 1991 when he announced that he had tested positive for the AIDS virus and was retiring from basketball. However, he played on the 1992 U.S. Olympic basketball team—the Dream Team—that won a gold medal. He then announced that he would return to the Lakers and began the 1992 NBA season with the team. However, his return caused a controversy, and he subsequently retired again after a few months.

In the closing months of the 1993–1994 season, Johnson became head coach of the Lakers. However, he didn't stay in the position long, citing frustration with the players' attitudes. Then, in another stunning turnaround, Johnson returned to the Lakers as a player for the 1996 season. When the team was eliminated in the first round of the playoffs, Johnson retired for the final time.

As a soccer player, **DIEGO ARMANDO MARADONA** wanted to do for Argentina what **Pelé** had done for Brazil. Although he scaled the heights of superstardom, he could not defeat the personal demons inside him.

He was born in Lanus near Buenos Aires, the fifth of eight children, and he began playing soccer for an Argentinian youth team when he was nine. At the age of sixteen, he became the youngest member of Argentina's national team. Although Maradona was a star in his country by 1978, he was left off the national team that year—the coach did not think he could handle the pressure of World Cup competition—and did not participate in Argentina's World Cup victory.

The following year, however, he was voted South American Player of the Year. From 1982–1984 he played for the Barcelona team in Spain. Maradona then led Argentina back to the World Cup and victory again in 1986. He was the most dominant player in

the tournament that year and was voted MVP of the event.

During the 1980s, Maradona also played for Napoli, an Italian team based in Naples. He helped them win the Italian Cup in 1987, the championship of the Italian League in 1987 and 1990, and the European Champion Clubs Cup in 1989.

At the pinnacle of his career, however, in March 1991, Maradona was hit with accusations of drug abuse. He was dropped from the Naples team and was suspended from international competition for fifteen months while he faced drug charges in Argentina.

In September 1992, Maradona seemed to be on the up-and-up, signing with Sevilla, another Spanish team. But he was only a shell of his former self and was dropped after one season.

Maradona said that the reason he struggled so mightily with Sevilla was because the training sessions were too much for him. He subsequently returned to Argentina for another comeback. However, during the World Cup of 1994, he was suspended again for fifteen months, this time testing positive for using ephedrine, a banned substance.

Maradona became coach of Racing Club, a soccer team from Argentina, but he quit in mid-1995. He then returned to playing, this time with the Boca Juniors team from Buenos Aires, before retiring for good in 1997. He served as a TV commentator in Argentina during the World Cup in 1998.

Despite his numerous problems that most certainly shortened his career, Maradona remains one of the most popular soccer players in history. In 2000, he was voted Fédération Internationale de Football Association (FIFA)'s Best Football Player of the Century in a worldwide poll on the internet.

GREG LOUGANIS was the first male diver in more than fifty years to win both the platform and the springboard events in the same Olympics. He then repeated those feats four years later, becoming the only male diver in the long history of the Olympic Games to win those events twice in succession.

Born to Samoan and Swedish parents, Louganis was given up for adoption by his teenage mother shortly after his birth. Raised in El Cajon, in Southern California, he had a difficult childhood. He was extremely shy as a youngster, primarily because of a reading disability, and classmates often hurled racial insults at him because of his dark skin.

However, Louganis found solace in dance classes, which he and his sister joined almost as soon as they could walk. In grade school, Louganis added gymnastics to his list of activities and progressed to diving. When he began doing gymnastic flips off the family diving board, his stepfather enrolled him in diving class.

At the age of eleven, he scored a perfect ten in the AAU Junior Olympics. Then, Louganis came under the tutelage of former Olympic diving gold medalist, Dr. **Sammy Lee**. When he was sixteen, Louganis participated in the 1976 Olympics and won a silver medal in platform diving.

By the spring of 1978, Louganis was emerging as a premier diver. That year, he won the world platform championship and the AAU indoor one-meter and three-meter titles. The next year, he won gold medals in both the springboard and the platform events at the Pan American Games.

It appears as if Louganis was primed and ready for the 1980 Olympics, but the United States boycotted the Moscow Games, and the dreams of all the athletes, including Louganis, were put on hold. After attending the University of Miami for three years, he switched colleges to get his bachelor's degree in drama from the University of California at Irvine in 1981, and to study under diving great **Ron O'Brien**.

In 1982, Louganis won both the platform and springboard diving events at the world championships. Two years later, at the Los Angeles Olympics, Louganis shone, winning gold medals in both diving events. He later won the Sullivan Award as the outstanding amateur athlete in America that year. In 1985, he was inducted into the U.S. Olympic Hall of Fame. Louganis repeated his double gold medal performance three more times at the 1986 world championships, the 1987 Pan American Games, and finally at the 1988 Olympics, despite hitting the springboard with his head. This secured his reputation as the greatest male diving champion in Olympics history.

After the 1988 Games, Louganis retired from competitive diving. In 1994, Greg came out to the world as gay, and the following year, disclosed that he had AIDS. He has continued to be a gay rights activist and HIV awareness advocate to keep people discussing these issues and to make a difference in the lives of others.

◆ The first gymnast in Olympic history to score perfect tens, tiny but mighty **NADIA COMĂNECI** won the hearts and minds of the sports world with her performance at the 1976 Olympics.

Comăneci was born in 1961 in Oneşti, Romania. She began gymnastics training early in life. When she was six years old, the great Romanian gymnastics teacher **Bela Karoli** spotted her while he was scouting public schools for potential members of the national junior gymnastics team.

In 1969, Comăneci entered national competition. The following year, she won the national junior championship. Karoli had coached her well. She continued winning competitions in her age group until 1975, when she began senior competition. That year, she entered the European championships and outclassed her competition, walking away with four of the five gold medals.

Despite her success, Comăneci was still a well-kept secret of the Eastern Bloc. That changed in 1976, when she came to North America for the first time before the Olympics in Montreal, Canada. In the qualifying meets for the Games, she registered perfect scores of 10.0 six out of eight times. She then won the American Cup competition, earning several more tens along the way. She was just fifteen years old and the talk of the sports world. Everybody loved the little girl with the graceful athleticism and flawless technique.

Then came the Olympics, where she became the first gymnast to receive a perfect score from the judges, earning all tens in the uneven bars event. She also won a gold medal in the all-around and in the balance beam, where she had a near-perfect point total of 19.95. In addition, she won a bronze medal in the floor exercise, and she led Romania to the silver medal in the team competition.

In the 1980 Olympics, Comăneci repeated her triumphs. She won gold medals in the balance beam and floor exercise events, and a silver in the all-around.

Comăneci defected from Romania to the United States on November 1, 1989. In 1996, she married American gymnast **Bart Conner**.

They called **WAYNE GRETZKY** the "**Great One**," and why not? During his twenty-year NHL career, he set more than sixty scoring records. He is perhaps the greatest hockey player to ever laced up a pair of skates.

Born in 1961, Gretzky was skating at the age of three on a backyard rink in his home in Brantford, Ontario, Canada. His dad drilled him in the essentials of hockey and did it so well that when Gretzky was six, he was competing against ten year olds.

During the 1977–1978 season, Gretzky played junior hockey with the Sault Sainte Marie Greyhounds of the Ontario Hockey League. Even though he was only a teenager, he scored 70 goals and had 122 assists in just sixty-four games.

In 1978, a few months shy of his eighteenth birthday, Gretzky signed a professional contract with the Indianapolis Racers of the WHA. He was the youngest athlete in North America to play on a major pro sports team. After eight games, the financially struggling Racers sold his contract to the WHA's Edmonton Oilers. Gretzky had an outstanding season for the Oilers, scoring 46 goals, adding 64 assists and being named the league's Rookie of the Year.

When the WHA folded and the Oilers moved to the NHL the following season, Gretzky became an immediate star. He amassed an amazing 137 points on 51 goals and 86 assists, winning the first of eight straight scoring titles.

However, Gretzky was just warming up. The following season, he set an NHL scoring record with 164 points. In the 1981–1982 season, he became the first player in NHL history to break the 200-point barrier when he tallied 120 assists and a record 92 goals for a total of 212 points.

Led by Gretzky, Edmonton became the NHL's most dominant team during the 1980s, winning four Stanley Cups during the decade. For his part, Gretzky won eight straight MVP awards during that period.

Despite their championships, by the late 1980s the Oilers were in financial difficulty, and in 1988, they traded Gretzky to the Los Angeles Kings. His presence immediately turned them from a weak franchise into a successful one, and although he was never able to bring a Stanley Cup to Los Angeles, Gretzky is credited with saving hockey in that city.

When he retired at the end of the 1998–1999 season, Gretzky held so many NHL records that it was hard to keep track of them all. Chief among them were career marks in goals with 894, assists with 1,963, and points with 2,857. The NHL fittingly retired Gretzky's jersey number 99, meaning that no other player would ever wear it.

American **GREG LEMOND** was a three-time winner of the prestigious Tour de France cycling race in an era when it was an accomplishment to just have an American in the race.

LeMond was born in Los Angeles, but his family moved to northwestern Nevada when he was a boy. There, his father developed an avid interest in long-distance cycling. Soon father and son were going on cycling trips together.

In 1975, LeMond joined the Reno, Nevada, Wheelman cycling club. In February 1976, he finished second in a twenty-five-mile race. In his first few months of competition, he won eleven races in his age group, then petitioned to be allowed to compete with sixteen to nineteen year olds. By year end, he had won the Nevada Junior championship and placed fourth in the Junior Nationals.

From that time on, LeMond devoted himself totally to cycling. He won the gold medal in the Junior Nationals in 1977, but it was in 1978 that LeMond stamped himself as an up-and-coming force in the cycling world. That year, he won gold, silver, and bronze medals at the Junior World Championships—the first time anyone had ever won three medals at that event.

In 1979, LeMond joined the Renault Gitane team in Europe, and he fell under the coaching tutelage of his teammate, the great French cyclist **Bernard Hinault** (see no 66).

In 1983, LeMond got his first major victory when he won a 169-mile road race in Switzerland with a superb time of 7:1:21. He also won the world professional road racing championship that year.

However, it was in the Tour de France that LeMond made his mark. His first attempt at this grueling race was in 1984, and despite a debilitating bout of bronchitis, he finished third—the best showing ever for a non-European cyclist. In the 1985 race, he finished second to Bernard Hinault. Finally, in 1986, LeMond broke through, beating Hinault by more than three minutes and becoming the first American to win the race.

A series of cycling accidents and a near fatal hunting accident in 1987 put LeMond's career on hold for a while, but in 1989, he won the Tour de France again—this time by a razor-thin margin of eight seconds. He also won the world professional road racing championship for the second time that year and was subsequently named Sportsman of the Year by *Sports Illustrated* magazine.

In 1990, LeMond won the Tour de France for the third time. However, in the early 1990s, a rare muscular disorder called mitochondrial myopathy was starting to take its toll on him. He retired from competitive cycling in 1994.

CARL LEWIS is one of the greatest all-around track-and-field athletes in modern history.

Born in Birmingham, Alabama, Lewis went to college at the University of Houston. He won the NCAA long jump championship in 1980 and qualified for the U.S. Olympic team that same year. However, when America boycotted the Games to protest the Soviet Union's invasion of Afghanistan, Lewis's Olympic dreams, like those of other U.S. athletes, were dashed for the moment.

Lewis did not slack on his training though, and in 1981, he won the NCAA and national outdoor 100-meter dash and long jump titles. He also won the Sullivan Award that year as the outstanding American amateur athlete.

Lewis continued his outstanding performances in 1982, and in 1983, at the track-and-field world championships in Finland, he won the 100-meter dash and the long jump. He was also a member of the winning 4 × 100-meter relay team.

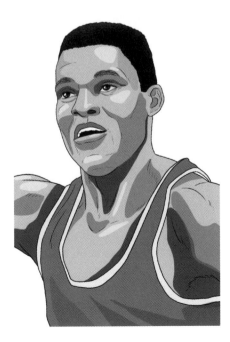

Then came the 1984 Olympics. Lewis put on a spectacular exhibition that year, winning gold medals in the 100- and 200-meter dashes, the long jump, and the 4 × 100-meter relay, duplicating the accomplishment of the immortal **Jesse Owens** in 1936. With his victory in the 100-meter dashes, Lewis earned the classic nickname as "world's fastest human."

Four years later, at the 1988 Olympics, Lewis won a gold medal in the long jump and another as a member of victorious 4 × 100-meter relay team. In the 100-meter dash, he ran a world record time of 9.93 seconds, but finished second to Canadian sprinter **Ben Johnson**. However, Johnson was subsequently found to have used banned substances and was disqualified, and as such, Lewis was declared the winner. Lewis also picked up a silver medal in the 200-meter dash.

At the 1991 World Athletics Championships in Japan, Lewis proved that he was still the world's fastest with a record time of 9.86 seconds in the 100-meter dash.

In 1992, Lewis continued his remarkable string of Olympic successes, although he did begin to slow down. Though he failed to qualify for either the 100- or 200-meter dashes, he did win a gold medal in the long jump and another as a member of the 4 × 100-meter relay team.

After Lewis hurt his back in a car accident in 1993, his continuation in athletic competition was in doubt. But he surprised naysayers by winning his fourth straight gold medal in the long jump at the 1996 Olympics. This gave him a staggering total of nine gold medals—only the fourth man to achieve this feat.

Lewis officially retired from track-and-field competition in 1997.

Other athletes may have more flash than **JACKIE JOYNER-KERSEE**, but few can match the accomplishments of one of the greatest female track stars of all time.

Jacqueline Joyner was born in East St. Louis, Illinois, in 1962. When she was twelve, she could broad jump more than seventeen feet. At the age of fourteen, she won the first of four consecutive United States junior national titles in the pentathlon. After she graduated from high school, she attended UCLA on a basketball scholarship. There, she met coach **Bob Kersee**, who she would marry in 1986.

In 1983, she and her brother Al, who was a triple jumper, represented the United States at the track-and-field world championships in Helsinki, Finland. The following year at the Olympics, she won the silver medal in the heptathlon—a grueling two-day event consisting of the 100-meter hurdles, the high jump, shot put, and the 200-meter on day one followed by the long jump, javelin, and the 800-meter race on day two. Sadly, she missed winning the gold medal by .06 seconds.

In 1985, she set an American record in the long jump at 23 feet, 9 inches. She set high point totals in several college meets in 1986, scoring 6,910 points at one and 6,841 at another. However, the 7,000-point barrier—a figure never reached by any single athlete—eluded her.

Later that year, though, at the Goodwill Games in Moscow, Joyner-Kersee became the first American woman to hold the world heptathlon record by tallying 7,148 points, shattering the world record by 200 points. She also set an American record of 12.85 seconds in the 100-meter hurdles, and a heptathlon mark of twenty-three feet in the long jump.

Less than a month later, at the U.S. Olympic Festival in Houston, she broke her own record with 7,161 points as well as breaking her American long jump record.

For her accomplishments, Joyner-Kersee was named the winner of the Sullivan Award as the country's top amateur athlete.

The victories for this amazing athlete kept coming. At the 1987 Pan American Games, she equaled the world record in the long jump. Then, in the track-and-field world championships, she won gold medals in the heptathlon with 7,128 points and the long jump with a distance of 24 feet and 1 3/4 inches.

Being hailed as "America's greatest athlete since **Jim Thorpe**," Joyner-Kersee won two gold medals at the 1988 Olympics—in the heptathlon and the long jump. She repeated her gold medal triumph in the heptathlon at the 1992 Olympics and also took home a bronze in the long jump. She became the first woman to win multi-event titles at two Olympics, and the first athlete overall to win multi-event medals at three Olympics. She was later voted the Greatest Female Athlete of the 20th Century by *Sports Illustrated*.

Playing at a position that has seen many great athletes over the years, **JERRY RICE** still stands out above all others. He is almost certainly the greatest wide receiver in pro football history.

A native of Starkville, Mississippi, Rice went to school at Mississippi Valley State University, where he became a star. Among the many records he set at the school was a total of 4,693 yards gained as a receiver. With credentials like that, Rice was destined to go fast in the 1985 NFL draft, and he did. He was nabbed up in the first round by the San Francisco 49ers—the sixteenth player drafted.

As a rookie, Rice had some problems holding onto the football, but by his second season, he began to fulfill the 49ers' high expectations of him. In 1986, he led the league with eighty-six receptions, piling up 1,520 yards, and scoring fifteen touchdowns. The following year, he set a single season record for the most touchdowns by a wide receiver with twenty-two. Remarkably, he set that record in a season that was shortened to just twelve games due to a player's strike.

Rice joined a team that had already won two Super Bowl championships in the 1980s, and his presence only added to its offensive weapons, which included quarterback **Joe Montana** and running back **Roger Craig**. "Montana-to-Rice" became a familiar cry in the NFL, and the duo led the team to back-to-back Super Bowl victories in 1989 and 1990, and Rice was named Super Bowl MVP in the 1989 game. In the early 1990s, when Montana was replaced by Steve Young, Rice became Young's favorite receiver, and the two led the team to another championship in 1995.

Rice became famous for his rigorous training regimen, which included running up the steps of football stadiums. That training kept him in terrific shape until a knee injury forced him to miss time in 1997. Before the injury, he had appeared in 189 consecutive games.

Rice played for the 49ers through the 1999 season, after which, in both an effort to save money and due to a belief that he was past his prime, the team let him go. However, Rice merely moved across the bay to the Oakland Raiders and continued baffling defensive backs.

By the time the 2002 season began, Rice held career records for most receptions, most receiving yards, most total touchdowns, and most consecutive games with a touchdown. In 2003, he made his thirteenth Pro Bowl appearance. Midway through the 2004 season, Rice was traded to the Seattle Seahawks, but he was released by the team at the end of the season. After an unsuccessful attempt to become a starting receiver for the Denver Broncos the following year, he signed a ceremonial one-day contract with San Francisco and retired as a 49er. Rice was inducted into the Pro Football Hall of Fame in 2010. Every time he put on his helmet and pads, he added more yardage to his many records, more detail to his legend, and more evidence to his being the greatest receiver of all time.

By near unanimous consensus, **MICHAEL JORDAN** is the greatest all-around pro basketball player in history.

Jordan was born in Brooklyn, New York, and his family moved to Wilmington, North Carolina, when he was very young. As a senior, he led his high school basketball team to nineteen wins and was recruited by legendary coach **Dean Smith** at the University of North Carolina at Chapel Hill (UNC). As a freshman, Jordan hit the winning basket with seconds left in the 1982 NCAA title game to deliver North Carolina the national championship. Jordan stayed at UNC two more years and was named College Player of the Year as a junior.

In 1984, the Chicago Bulls of the NBA selected Jordan as the third overall pick in the draft, and he immediately revitalized the franchise. In his first year, he led the team in points per game with 28.2, rebounds with 6.5, assists with 5.9, and steals with 2.4. He was named Rookie of the Year and was an All-Star, but the Bulls were eliminated in the playoffs.

That was the pattern of Jordan's first few years with the Bulls—great individual play, such as when he scored sixty-three points in a game or scored over 3,000 points in a season—but team failure in the playoffs.

All that changed, however, when **Phil Jackson** became the Bulls' head coach. With Jackson at the helm, the Bulls won three straight NBA championships, in 1991, 1992 and 1993.

In 1993, Jordan decided he wanted a career change, so he abandoned basketball to play baseball, signing with the Chicago White Sox minor league team. However, after this brief stint, Jordan returned to basketball, and the Bulls reeled off three more consecutive NBA championship wins.

Jordan was a unique player, a man who seemed to defy gravity as he soared through the air to make impossible shots or snatch rebounds. His popularity and commercial appeal were unlimited, and he is credited with pumping up interest in pro basketball to an all-time peak.

In 1998, Jordan retired again. When he left, he had scored 29,277 points and amassed 5,836 rebounds. He held the NBA record for the highest career scoring average with 31.5 points for 10 seasons. He was a five-time league MVP, a six-time MVP of the championship finals, and a perennial NBA All-Star.

After two inactive years, the lure of the game proved too much to resist, and Jordan came back in 2001 to play with the Washington Wizards. Although age and injuries had robbed him of some of his amazing ability, he still showed flashes of the old Michael Jordan on the court. Knowing that the 2002–2003 season would be his last in the NBA, fans, teammates, opponents, and officials gave him an emotional three-minute standing ovation after his last game on April 16, 2003, and the world said goodbye to the game's greatest player. In 2009, he was inducted into the Basketball Hall of Fame.

Speed skater **BONNIE BLAIR** has won more Olympic gold medals than any other American female athlete.

Although she was born in Cornwall, New York, she grew up in Champaign, Illinois—the unofficial speed skating capital in the United States. All six Blair children skated competitively, and four of Blair's siblings grew up to be national champions.

At the age of six, Blair won races against nine- and ten-year-old girls. At seven, she competed in the short track speed skating state championships. In 1979, Blair met Olympic gold medalist and speed skating coach **Cathy Faminow**, who encouraged her to work on her speed skating year-round. In 1980, Blair decided to concentrate on Olympic-style racing—in which two skaters are on the track, racing against time rather than one another—instead of the short track.

Even though she was nationally ranked, in 1982, Blair was advised to train in Europe. She was short of funds, so the local police department hosted a series of raffles and bake sales so she could raise the money. Blair received much needed experience in Olympic-style skating during her time in Europe.

Blair won the U.S. indoor title in 1983, 1984, and 1986, and was the North American indoor champion in 1985. After setting a world record time in the 500-meter event at the 1987 world championships, Blair was ready for the Winter Olympic Games the following year.

In the 1988 Games in Calgary, Canada, Blair won the gold medal in the 500-meter race with a blazing time of 39.1 seconds. When she also won the bronze medal in the 1,000-meter race, she became the only American athlete to win more than one medal at that year's Olympics.

However, Blair's Olympic triumphs were just beginning. At the 1992 Games, she again won the 500-meter race and also picked up a gold in the 1,000-meter race, which she won by only two hundredths of a second. She also became the first woman from any nation to win consecutive gold medals in the 500-meter race.

Then in 1994, at the Games in Lillehammer, Norway, she did it again, winning the gold medal in both the 500-meter and 1,000-meter races. This gave her five golds—more than any other American female Olympic athlete. With her six medals, she surpassed **Eric Heiden's** Winter Olympics medal record of five, giving her the most medals of any U.S. Winter Olympian.

Blair earned other honors as well during her career. In 1992, she received the Sullivan Award, which is given to one outstanding American amateur athlete each year.

In 1995, Blair retired from competitive skating.

TONY HAWK'S older brother got him into the sport in the 1970s, when he gave him an old skateboard at the age of nine and started taking him to skate parks. "I literally saw people flying. Like, I saw these guys flying out of empty swimming pools. And that was my 'wow' moment. Where I was like, I want to do whatever they're doing," Hawk said.

Born in 1968 in San Diego, California, Hawk was a boy who did not like failure. It did not take long for the nine-year-old learning at the skate park to turn into a fourteen-year-old, who had already gone pro. By sixteen, he was seen by many as the best skateboarder in the world. According to his website, by the age of twenty-five, he had won seventy-three contests and was attracting a steady stream of sponsorship deals.

During the 1980s and 1990s, he dominated skateboarding competitions. He was named the top vert (vertical) skater every year from 1984 to 1996. He also invented dozens of moves, including the ollie-to-Indy,

the gymnast plant, the frontside 540-rodeo flip, and the Saran wrap. In one of skateboarding's defining moments, Hawk executed a 900 twist (2 1/2 turns) at the 1999 **X Games**, a move that had never been performed before.

In the early 1990s, Hawk started Birdhouse, a skateboard and accessories manufacturer, and Blitz, a skateboard products distributor. The companies were both successful, and he soon became involved in other ventures. In 1998, he and his family created a line of children's skate clothing called Hawk Clothing, and that same year, he began to develop a skateboard-themed video game. *Tony Hawk's Pro Skater* debuted in 1999, and it made more than $1 billion in sales. Hawk had become an entire brand.

Though Hawk retired from competition in 1999, he remained active in promoting the sport and his products. In 2002, he created *Tony Hawk's Boom Boom HuckJam*, a traveling show of choreographed skateboarders, BMX bikers, motorcycle stunt riders, and popular punk bands. That year, the Tony Hawk Foundation was founded to help develop skate parks in low-income neighborhoods. Hawk also wrote several books on skateboarding, and his autobiography, *Hawk: Occupation: Skateboarder* (cowritten with Sean Mortimer), was published in 2000. Hawk was even trending in the summer of 2021 when he sold 100 boards made with red paint that actually contained his blood. The boards sold out almost immediately. It doesn't get much cooler than that!

Tony Hawk brought skateboarding into the mainstream as a recognized sport in the 1990s, and his legacy has helped it stay there ever since.

The word "courageous" can be defined in several different ways, but surely that word can be applied to **LANCE ARMSTRONG**, the American cyclist who won the Tour de France a record-tying seven times.

He was born in Plano, Texas, and mainly raised by his mother. Armstrong was attracted to athletics at an early age, and by the age of thirteen he was competing in triathlons—events comprising cycling, swimming, and running. Three years later, he was good enough to turn professional.

Cycling was proving more alluring than swimming or running, however, and Armstrong soon devoted all his energy to it. The national cycling club took notice of this dedicated youngster and invited him to work with them while he was a senior in high school.

Armstrong qualified for the 1989 Junior World Championships in Moscow in the summer following his high school graduation. Two years later, he won the U.S. Amateur Championships. He also won two other cycling races that year—the First Union Grand Prix and the Thrifty Drug Classic.

In August 1993, Armstrong became the youngest man in history to win the world road race championship in Oslo, Norway. The following year, he was runner-up in the Tour DuPont, which he then won in 1995 by posting the largest margin of victory in its history.

Armstrong soon was facing a challenge beyond any mere cycling race. In October 1996, after signing a lucrative sponsorship contract, he learned that he had testicular cancer, which had spread to his brain and lungs. He was given a forty-percent chance of recovery, and he subsequently lost his sponsorship contract.

It was then that Armstrong showed what he was made of. Thanks to a rigorous chemotherapy program and surgery, he was pronounced healthy in February 1997. He then began training, determined to scale the heights of the cycling world once again. With the sponsorship muscle of the U.S. Postal Service behind him, Armstrong won several races in 1998 as he slowly climbed back into the competitive cycling mainstream.

Then in 1999, Armstrong wrote the sweetest possible conclusion to his comeback story by winning the world's premier bicycle race, the Tour de France. This was just the first of his five successive victories in the event—tying the career record for wins held by four other cyclists and equaling the consecutive win record of **Miguel Indurain**.

After he was diagnosed with cancer, Armstrong established the Lance Armstrong Foundation, which has helped to advance cancer research, diagnosis, treatment, and after-treatment services. Having beaten his cancer, Armstrong wanted to help others succeed in this toughest fight of all.

Between 2000 and 2005, Armstrong won the Tour de France six more times and retired in 2005. In 2009, he returned to cycling and retired again in 2011. Sadly, the world began to suspect that Armstrong had possibly been using illegal performance-enhancing drugs in order to win, and in 2013, in an interview with talk show host Oprah Winfrey, Armstrong finally admitted to using these drugs during each Tour de France win from 1999–2005. After this revelation, Armstrong was stripped of his titles and received a lifetime ban from all sports.

The U.S. women's soccer team is one of the best soccer teams ever, but before there was Megan Rapinoe, Alex Morgan, and Carli Lloyd, there was **MIA HAMM**. Mia Hamm is thought by many to be the best female soccer player in history. She competed with the national U.S. women's soccer team for seventeen years and won the Women's World Cup in 1991 and 1999 while winning Olympic gold medals in 1996 and 2004.

Hamm was born in 1972 in Selma, Alabama. Playing soccer as a teenager, she drew attention for her talent for scoring goals. When she was fifteen, she was the youngest person ever to become a member of the U.S. team. She went to college at UNC Chapel Hill, and after she graduated in 1994, helped the Tarheels win four NCAA championships.

Back in 1991, at the age of nineteen, Hamm was the youngest U.S. team member in history to win the **World Cup**. Five years later, Hamm and her teammates earned the gold medal at the 1996 Summer Olympics in

Atlanta, Georgia, and they would return to win gold again in 2004. In 1999, Hamm set a record for most international goals scored when she made her 108th goal for the U.S. team.

Hamm's other achievements include being elected Soccer USA's Female Athlete of the Year five years in a row (1994–1998), being named MVP of the Women's Cup (1995) and winning three Excellence in Sports Performance Yearly Award (ESPY) Awards, including in the Soccer Player of the Year and Female Athlete of the Year categories. In 2004, she and teammate Michelle Akers were named on FIFA's list of the 125 Greatest Living Soccer Players—becoming the only women and the only Americans named on the list at that time.

With Hamm as the star, the U.S. women's team enjoyed unprecedented media attention for a women's sports team, especially during the 1999 World Cup held in the United States. Shirts with her number "9" became a top-selling item, and her popularity, which continues into her retirement, rivaled that of the best-known male athletes.

After retiring from competitive play in 2004, she remained involved in the sport. In 2014 Hamm became co-owner with her husband, former baseball player Nomar Garciaparra, and others of the Major League Soccer's Los Angeles Football Club (FC), which began play in 2018. In 2020, she became co-owner of Angel City FC, a new Los Angeles-based team in the National Women's Soccer League.

In a sport filled with legendary names and careers—Jones, Nicklaus, Palmer—the name of **TIGER WOODS** might one day be the most legendary of all.

Eldrick Woods was born in 1975 in Orange County, California. He was nicknamed "Tiger" after a Vietnamese soldier, who was a friend of his father. When he was ten months old, he would watch his father hit golf balls into a net for hours. Like a true child prodigy, when he was three years old, he shot a 48 for nine holes. Two years later, he was featured in *Golf Digest* magazine.

When Woods was seven, his father had him listening to subliminal tapes to improve his mental game. His father would also try his hardest to distract Woods while he was swinging in order to teach him mental toughness.

Woods attended Stanford University and played on the golf team. Along the way, he won numerous amateur tournaments. He won the U.S. Junior Amateur three years in a row from 1991–1993 when no one before had ever won more than one. He was named the top amateur player by *Golf Digest*, *Golfweek*, and *Golf World* in 1992 and 1993. In 1996, he won the NCAA championship and was the Collegiate Player of the Year.

In 1996, Woods turned pro and immediately had success, notching two victories and three top ten finishes in his first eight starts. His first PGA win came at the Las Vegas Invitational. That year, he was the PGA Tour Rookie of the Year. He was also named *Sports Illustrated*'s Sportsman of the Year.

Since then, Woods has become the most dominant player in professional golf. In 1997, he was the PGA Tour Player of the Year, winning four tournaments and finishing in the top ten in nine others. He also set a 72-hole record at the Masters Tournament with a 270. In 1999, Woods earned over $6 million, nearly three million more than his nearest competitor.

The following year, Woods had one of the greatest seasons in golf history. He won the U.S. Open and British Open tournaments, as well as the PGA championship, giving him all four Grand Slam titles at the unbelievable age of twenty-five. He won nine PGA tournaments and earned a record of more than $8 million.

By the year 2002, Woods had won eight Grand Slam tournaments. In 2004, Woods got married, and the couple had their first child in 2007. Their second child was born in 2009, but later that year news broke that Woods had crashed his car outside his home. He only suffered minor injuries, but his personal life began to unravel shortly after the crash, and he and his wife divorced in 2010. It wasn't until the 2012 Arnold Palmer Invitational that Tiger would see another golf win. He also endured many different back surgeries in the years that followed that had a major impact on his game and career.

Woods did come back to win the Tour Championship in 2018, and in 2019, he won the Masters for the fifth time. In 2020, Woods received another back surgery, and in 2021, he suffered serious leg injuries after another car accident. After recovering, Woods acknowledged that though he would continue competing in a few events per year, his full-time golf career was over.

LAILA ALI, an undefeated boxing world champion, cares a lot about helping others discover fitness and wellness. Ali is also a TV host, home chef, founder of the Laila Ali Lifestyle brand, and mom. She is the daughter of late champion and humanitarian **Muhammad Ali**, and her record includes twenty-four wins (twenty-one of which were knockouts) and zero losses. She is seen as the most successful woman in the history of women's boxing.

Ali was born in 1977 in Miami Beach, Florida, the second youngest of Muhammad Ali's nine children. She didn't always set out to be a boxer. She went to college for business management and owned a nail salon. Soon though, she was inspired to start training as a boxer after watching a televised fight between two women's boxers in 1996. And in 1999, she made her professional boxing ring debut, and this fight attracted major media attention. Ali became a reason for the world to focus on women's boxing. The power of the Ali family name, which brings memories of a remarkable fighter whose skills and personality captivated millions of boxing fans, is undeniable.

She knocked out her opponent thirty-one seconds into the first round. Over the next eight years, she faced off against many leading names in women's boxing. In 2001, she defeated Jacqui Frazier-Lyde, daughter of boxer **Joe Frazier**. In a nod to the long-standing competition between the two women's fathers, the fight was publicized as "Ali vs. Frazier IV."

In 2002, Ali was named Super Middleweight Champion by the International Boxing Association, the Women's International Boxing Association, and the International Women's Boxing Federation. Two years later, she added the International Women's Boxing Federation's Light Heavyweight title to her résumé.

Ali's final fight took place on February 3, 2007, in Johannesburg, South Africa. She knocked out opponent **Gwendolyn O'Neil** in the first round, finishing her career with a 24–0 record that included twenty-one knockouts.

Ali promotes equality for women in the world of professional sports and programs that encourage young women to be confident, healthy, and strong through sports.

Known for her consistency and artistry on the ice, **MICHELLE KWAN** made history as the most decorated American figure skater of all time, a five-time world champion, and a nine-time U.S. champion. She is considered by many to be one of the greatest figure skaters of all time.

Kwan was born in Torrance, California, in 1980. Her parents were Chinese immigrants from Hong Kong, and Kwan grew up speaking both English and Cantonese at home. When she was young, both of Kwan's older siblings were involved in ice sports: her brother Ron played ice hockey and her sister Karen figure skated, which helped spark Kwan's own interest in figure skating when she was five years old. When she was eight, she and her sister began serious training, arriving at the rink at 5 a.m. to practice before school, and returning after school to continue practicing. When Kwan was ten, she and her sister began training at the Ice Castle International Training Center in Lake Arrowhead, California. After just one year, Kwan placed ninth in the junior level at the United States Figure Skating Championships.

In 1992, at the age of twelve, Kwan qualified to compete as a senior-level skater, and in 1993, she placed sixth at her first senior U.S. Championships. The following year, she won the World Junior Championships. At the U.S. Championships in 1994, Kwan finished second behind Tonya Harding and was sent to the 1994 Olympic Games as an alternate.

After struggles with her lutz jump landed her second place at the 1995 U.S. Championships, Kwan began to refine her style. She improved her speed and jump technique and began taking on more difficult choreography, grabbing first-place finishes at both the U.S. Championships and the World Championships in 1996. After winning the U.S. title again in 1998 despite competing with a fractured toe, Kwan was favored to win gold at the 1998 Olympics in Nagano, Japan, but ended up placing second behind U.S. teammate Tara Lipinski. Kwan went on to win the World Championships for a second time later that same year.

Kwan successfully defended her U.S. and World Championship titles in 2000 and again in 2001. She won the U.S. Championships again yet again in 2002. However, Olympic gold once again eluded her in Salt Lake City that year when she placed third behind U.S. teammate Sarah Hughes and Russian skater Irina Slutskaya.

Kwan continued competing, steadily increasing the difficulty of her routines. She won the World Championships again in 2003, and the U.S. Championships in 2003, 2004, and 2005. Despite fighting through injuries during the season, Kwan made it to Turin in 2006 to compete again for Olympic gold. But after suffering another injury during her first practice in Turin, Kwan withdrew from the games.

After the disappointment in Turin, Kwan decided to focus on her education, completing her undergraduate degree at the University of Denver in 2009. She ultimately decided to pursue graduate studies and a career in diplomacy.

Kwan was inducted into the World Figure Skating Hall of Fame in 2012.

SERENA WILLIAMS is a record-breaking tennis champion who has always had big dreams. She has won about every title there is, but that has never been enough. Serena is a philanthropist and a businessperson with a clothing and jewelry line. She has been in movies and music videos and has an award-winning docuseries that inspires people around the world. And she is a mother. Serena's life is as big as her dreams.

American woman after Althea Gibson in 1958 to win a Grand Slam singles tournament. Since then, Serena has dominated.

She has seventeen singles Grand Slam titles, fifteen doubles Grand Slam titles, and two mixed doubles Grand Slam titles. In the women's singles category, she has won five U.S. Open, five Wimbledon, five Australian Open, and two French Open titles. In the women's doubles category, along with her sister Venus, she has won

Williams was born in 1981 in Saginaw, Michigan, the youngest of five daughters. Serena's sister **Venus** would also become a great tennis champion. Serena's parents wanted to see their daughters succeed, so they moved to Compton, California, where Serena worked hard through long daily practices with her father and played on courts that were often filled with potholes and sometimes missing nets. She learned to play tough in a tough environment. By 1991, she was ranked first in the 10-and-under division of the junior U.S. association tour. At that time, her family moved again to Florida. Their father decreased their playing time in the junior tournament schedule to focus on practicing and to avoid seeing his daughters burn out. Serena was enrolled at the Rick Macci Tennis Academy and stayed there until 1995, the year she then turned pro. Within two short years, her ranking went from 304 to 99, and she received her first $12 million shoe deal with Puma. Williams won the U.S. Open, her first Grand Slam title, in 1999. This made her the second African

two U.S. Open, five Wimbledon, four Australian Open, and two French Open titles. She also won three Olympic gold medals in 2000, 2008, and 2012, making her the sixth woman in the open era to complete a career Grand Slam.

Serena is a competitor and has played against her older sister Venus in a total of twenty-five professional matches, with a win-loss record of 14–11. This includes eight Grand Slam finals, of which Serena has won six. Between 2002–2003, the sisters faced off in four consecutive Grand Slam finals, all of which were won by Serena. She is currently ranked fourth in overall singles titles with a total of seventeen, ranking behind Steffi Graf with twenty-two titles and Chris Evert and Martina Navratilova with eighteen titles each.

Williams has won over $50 million so far in her career, the highest of any female athlete and the fourth highest among tennis athletes of all time. Simply put, Serena Williams is a true champion, and she has no plans to stop anytime soon.

In 2015, **MISTY COPELAND** became the first African American ballerina to be appointed as a principal dancer for the prestigious **American Ballet Theatre (ABT)**.

Born in Kansas City, Missouri, in 1982 and raised in San Pedro, California, Copeland was the fourth of six siblings. She grew up moving several times and suffering emotional and physical abuse from men associated with her mother. Misty was an anxious child who found peace in the halls of school.

Misty Copeland began her ballet studies at the age of thirteen at the San Pedro City Ballet. At the age of fifteen, she won first place in the Music Center Spotlight Awards. She then began studying at the Lauridsen Ballet Center. Copeland has studied at the San Francisco Ballet School and American Ballet Theatre's Summer Intensive on full scholarship and was declared ABT's National Coca-Cola Scholar in 2000.

Copeland joined ABT Studio Company in September 2000, then joined American Ballet Theatre as a member of the corps de ballet in April 2001 and was appointed a soloist in August 2007. She has had many roles with the company. Copeland received the 2008 Leonore Annenberg Fellowship in the Arts and was named National Youth of the Year Ambassador for the Boys & Girls Clubs of America in 2013. In 2014, President Obama appointed Copeland to the President's Council on Fitness, Sports, and Nutrition. She is the recipient of a 2014 *Dance* Magazine Award and was named to the 2015 Time 100 by *Time* magazine. Copeland is the author of the best-selling memoir, *Life in Motion*, children's book *Firebird*, and health and fitness title, *Ballerina Body*.

Copeland has acknowledged the responsibility she feels to brown girls looking to make their way in the art form. Her trailblazing accomplishments have been recognized by a range of institutions, and in spring 2015, she was named one of *Time*'s 100 Most Influential People—a rare feat for someone from the dance world. In June 2015, Copeland became the first African American woman to dance with ABT in the dual role of Odette and Odile in Pyotry Ilycih Tchaikovsky's *Swan Lake*. Then on June 30 of that same year, Copeland scored a monumental achievement that covered the world over, becoming the first African American performer to be appointed an ABT principal dancer in the company's seventy-five-year history. At a subsequent news conference, an emotional Copeland stated in tears that the announcement marked the culmination of her lifelong dream.

Many people claim **LEBRON JAMES** to be one of the best basketball players today, maybe even of all time. He is certainly among the top players and has been proving it ever since he was drafted to the NBA directly out of high school in 2003.

James was born in 1984 in Akron, Ohio, and at an early age, displayed a natural talent for basketball. He was recruited by St. Vincent–St. Mary High School to join their basketball team in 1999. Overall, James scored 2,657 points, 892 rebounds, and 523 assists during his four years there.

As a freshman, James averaged eighteen points per game. He helped the team to a Division III state title by scoring twenty-five points in the championship game. Word of his skills spread, and James received several honors for his performance. As a high school sophomore, James was chosen for USA Today's All-USA First Team Award. He was the first sophomore ever selected for this award. His team also won the Division III state title for the second year in a row. The following school year, James was named *Parade* magazine's High School Boys Basketball Player of the Year and Gatorade Player of the Year. James had a tremendous senior year on the court. He averaged 31.6 points per game, helping his team clinch their third state title. The St. Vincent–St. Mary High School team also earned the top national ranking that year.

The Cleveland Cavaliers signed James, and he proved to be a valuable addition to the struggling team. He played his first seven seasons with Cleveland. Despite his talent, the team was not able to win a championship, and in 2010, James switched teams and went to the Miami Heat.

During his four years with the Miami Heat, LeBron led the team to the NBA championship finals every year, winning twice.

In 2014, James moved back to Cleveland because he wanted to bring a championship to his hometown. The Cavaliers made it to the championship in 2014, but lost when two of their star players, Kevin Love and Kyrie Irving, went down due to injury. LeBron finally brought the NBA title to Cleveland in 2016.

In 2018, James announced that he was moving on to the Los Angeles Lakers. Together, the team struggled at first, but then soon began a turnaround. In the 2019–2020 season, the Lakers won the NBA championship, making James' fourth personal championship and fourth Finals MVP Award.

A philanthropist, he is an active supporter of the Boys & Girls Club of America, the Children's Defense Fund, and ONEXONE. He has also established his own charity foundation called the LeBron James Family Foundation. LeBron James is a true champion and does not plan to stop anytime soon.

MICHAEL PHELPS is quite possibly the greatest swimmer of all time. At the very least, he is certainly a prodigy. Some might even say he is also the greatest Olympian ever because he holds the record for the most Olympic medals won by anyone: twenty-eight medals in total with twenty-three being gold medals. None of the other great Olympians have even close to that number.

Phelps was born in 1985 in Baltimore, Maryland the youngest of three children. He started taking swim lessons at age seven because his older sisters were swimmers. At first, he was scared to put his head underwater, so his early instructors let him just float around on his back. The backstroke was the first stroke he mastered. By the age of ten, he held a national record for his age group in the 100-meter butterfly and began to train at the North Baltimore Aquatic Club. By 1999, Phelps made the U.S. national team. In 2000, he was at the Olympic Games in Sydney at age fifteen.

He would dominate the next four Olympic Games, finishing the most decorated athlete at each one. In 2004 at Athens, he won six golds and two bronzes, and Beijing 2008 would see the greatest ever number of medals won by a single athlete in an Olympic Games when Phelps won eight golds and broke world records while earning seven of them. At London 2012, he racked up four golds and two silvers, and then retired briefly, but came back for Rio 2016 at age thirty-one to win five gold medals and one silver. Overall, Phelps has set thirty-nine world records—the most of all time.

Michael Phelps' life has not been only about winning and awards. After the London Olympics, several aspects of his life were becoming overwhelming and the pressure of everything manifested into a problem with alcohol. Phelps was caught up in issues involved with success and stardom, with his father, and with his parents' divorce. He was drinking and partying too much and was arrested for charges of drinking and driving. His family helped him seek out rehab, and he spent much time getting back in touch with himself and his goals.

At the Rio Olympics in 2016, he added six medals—five golds—to his overall total. He retired permanently after the 2016 games. Today, his focus is on the importance of mental health and wellness. He works for his own charitable foundation, The Michael Phelps Foundation, focusing on the mental health of children.

Olympian and two-time FIFA Women's World Cup Champion **MEGAN RAPINOE** is known not only for her amazing assists and goals but also for her fierce activism for LGBTQ rights and racial and gender equality.

Born in 1985 in Redding, California, Rapinoe grew up as one of seven siblings. She started playing soccer when she was three after seeing her older brother Brian play.

During high school, she and her twin sister Rachael played soccer for Elk Grove Pride, a club team in the Women's Premier Soccer League (WPSL) two and a half hours away from her hometown. In 2005, Rapinoe and her sister both entered the University of Portland on soccer scholarships and led Portland to win the Division I title that year.

Rapinoe's sophomore and junior season ended early due to ACL injuries, but after recovering, she was named West Coast Conference Player of the Year as a senior and entered the Women's Professional Soccer Draft in 2009. The forward was selected as second overall by the Chicago Red Stars. After short stints with teams in Australia and France, Rapinoe joined Seattle Reign FC in 2013, where she was the top scorer in 2013 and 2017.

Many of Rapinoe's most amazing feats occurred while playing with the U.S. Women's National Team. She debuted with the team in 2006 and scored her first two goals with them that same year. After recovering from her ACL injuries, she returned to the team in 2009, participating in her first FIFA Women's World Cup in 2011. She stunned onlookers when, during the quarterfinal game against Brazil, she passed the ball in an impressive cross straight to teammate Abby Wambach, who then scored and tied the game just before the clock ran out. Though the U.S. team went on to place second in the tournament, they took gold at the 2012 Olympics, where Rapinoe became the first player ever to achieve an Olimpico (a goal scored directly from a corner kick) at an Olympic Games. Rapinoe helped lead the U.S. women to victory at the 2015 World Cup, and again at the 2019 World Cup, where she was awarded the Golden Boot as the top scorer of the tournament, and the Golden Ball as the best overall player. That same year, she was awarded the Ballon d'Or Féminin award.

Rapinoe is also known for her activism. She publicly came out as a lesbian in July 2012 in an effort to empower others in the LGBTQ community. In September 2016, she became one of the first athletes on a national stage to kneel during the national anthem in solidarity with **Colin Kaepernick** (see no. 99) and in protest of police brutality and racial injustice. In March 2019, she was one of twenty-seven members of the U.S. women's soccer team who collectively filed a lawsuit against the United States Soccer Federation, accusing it of gender discrimination. The lawsuit claimed that the U.S. women's team players were treated differently than the men's team—including being provided inferior training facilities, medical treatment, and being paid less than the U.S. men's team—despite the women winning more games and championships and making it further in tournaments than the men's team. The lawsuit was dismissed in May 2020 by a federal judge, and after working on an appeal, Rapinoe and her teammates reached an agreement with U.S. Soccer in December 2020 to improve working conditions and strive toward equal pay for the U.S. women's team players.

ALLYSON FELIX

b. 1985

World champion and Olympian **ALLYSON FELIX** made history as the most decorated woman in U.S. track-and-field history.

Felix was born in Los Angeles, California, in 1985, the daughter of an ordained minister and an elementary school teacher. After trying out for track-and-field in ninth grade, Felix quickly discovered her athletic talent, achieving her first international title in 2001 at the Debrecan World Youth Championships, where she won the 100-meter sprint. In her senior year of high school, she finished second in the 200-meter dash at the U.S. Indoor Track and Field Championships. When she graduated from high school in 2003, Felix chose to sign a professional contract with Adidas rather than compete at the collegiate level, though Adidas paid for her tuition at the University of Southern California.

At the age of eighteen, Felix earned a silver medal in the 200-meter event at the 2004 Olympics in Athens and set a world junior record with her time of 22.18 seconds. In 2005, she became the youngest gold medalist in the 200-meter dash at the Helsinki World Championships, and won gold again in 2007 in Osaka, in the 4 × 100-meter and 4 × 400-meter relays. Felix won silver again in the 200-meter dash at the 2008 Olympics in Beijing, finishing in 21.93 seconds, but won gold with the 4 × 400-meter relay team. Felix won her first individual Olympic gold medal at the 2012 Olympic Games in London for the 200-meter event, and won gold again in the 4 × 100-meter and 4 × 400-meter relays, becoming the first American woman to win three golds at an Olympics since **Florence Griffith Joyner** (see no. 72) twenty-four years prior.

After suffering a hamstring injury, Felix was unable to compete for nine months, and when she returned in 2014, she began competing in the individual 400-meter race, as well as the 200-meter sprint. She won the 400-meter event at the 2015 USATF Outdoor Championships, and won in the same event a few months later at the world championships. At the 2016 Olympics, Felix earned a silver medal in the 400-meter race, and gold in the 4 × 100-meter and 4 × 400-meter relays, growing her medal count to nine and becoming the most decorated woman in U.S. track-and-field history.

Felix reduced her racing schedule in 2018, and in November that year, she gave birth to her daughter prematurely. In May 2019, Felix made news by accusing her longtime sponsor Nike of refusing to guarantee salary protections for female athletes after giving birth. Nike soon altered their policy to ensure salary protections for athletes during pregnancy and as new mothers.

After training during the COVID-19 pandemic, Felix competed in her fifth and final Olympics in 2021. Despite some doubt that she would medal due to her age and slower-than-usual qualifying times, Felix claimed bronze in the 400-meter race, running 49.46 seconds, and the gold in the 4 × 400-meter relay. These results brought her medal count to eleven, officially making her the most decorated track-and-field athlete in Olympic history.

Known for his incredible international wins and record-setting races, Jamaican athlete **USAIN BOLT** is widely regarded as the greatest sprinter of all time.

Born Usain St. Leo Bolt in 1986 in Montego Bay, Jamaica, and grew up playing cricket and street football with his brother. Despite wanting to play other sports, Bolt was encouraged to try track-and-field events by his cricket coach, who had seen Bolt's sprint potential. In 2001, Bolt won his first annual high school championship medal, placing second in the 200-meter dash. Bolt made his world debut later that year at the International Association of Athletics Federations (IAAF) World Youth Championships in Hungary.

By the time he was fifteen, Bolt had grown to be six feet, five inches tall, and stood out at the 2002 World Junior Championships held in Kingston, Jamaica. Competing in front of a home crowd made him so nervous that he put his shoes on the wrong feet before his race, though he noticed his mistake and fixed them before the event. He won the 200-meter event with a time of 20.61 seconds, becoming the youngest world junior gold medalist ever. He also won two silver medals as a member of the Jamaican sprint relay team for the 4 × 100-meter and 4 × 400-meter relays, soon becoming known as "Lightning Bolt."

After winning gold at the 2003 World Youth Championships and breaking 200-meter and 400-meter race time records in his final Jamaican High School Championships, Bolt was chosen for the 2004 Jamaican Olympic team. However, a leg injury caused him to be eliminated in the first round of the 200-meter run. Despite being offered track scholarships to American colleges, Bolt chose to remain in Jamaica and continue training there.

Despite reaching global Top 5 rankings in 2005 and 2006, injuries sidelined him for much of those seasons. He returned to major competition in 2007, winning a silver medal in the 200-meter dash at the world championships in Osaka, Japan. Motivated by his second-place finish and his desire to compete in the 100-meter dash, Bolt grew more serious about his career and training. In May 2008, at the Reebok Grand Prix in New York City, Bolt ran the 100-meter dash in 9.72 seconds and went onto the Beijing Olympics just a few months later, holding a new world record. In the 100-meter Olympic final, Bolt improved his own record, winning the race in just 9.69 seconds—a massive 0.2 seconds ahead of second-place finisher Richard Thompson. A few days later, he took gold in the 200-meter final, setting both world and Olympic records in the event at 19.30 seconds. This made him the first sprinter in more than thirty years to hold both the 100-meter and 200-meter records simultaneously. He set yet another record two days later when he ran the third leg in the Jamaican 4 × 100-meter relays team, with the team finishing after 37.10 seconds and collecting gold.

Bolt was similarly successful at the 2012 and 2016 Olympic Games, again winning consecutive gold medals in the 100-meter dash, the 200-meter dash, and the 4 × 100 relay, and successfully defending his records.

Bolt retired from sprinting as an undisputed legend, leaving his sport as an eight-time Olympic gold medalist, eleven-time world champion, and world record holder several times over.

Known as a trailblazer for women in martial arts, **RONDA "ROWDY" ROUSEY** is widely viewed as one of the defining athletes of the twenty-first century.

Rousey was born in 1987 in Riverside, California, the youngest of three daughters. As a young child, Rousey suffered from apraxia, a condition that caused her to struggle with speech.

When she was eleven, Rousey began learning judo. She trained for two years with her mother AnnMaria De Mars, a champion judoka, until Rousey accidentally broke her mother's wrist. When Rousey was seventeen, she became the youngest judoka to qualify for the 2004 Olympic Games in Athens, and later the year she went on to win gold at the World Junior Judo Championships in Hungary. At the age of nineteen, she won bronze at the Junior World Championships, making her the first U.S. athlete to win two Junior World medals. Rousey also made history in 2008 at the Olympic Games in Beijing, where she won bronze and became the first American woman to medal in Olympic judo.

After Beijing, Rousey made her amateur mixed martial arts debut in 2010, heavily incorporating her judo skills of grounding her opponents with grappling and throwing, and then finishing with strikes or submissions. In her debut fight, she defeated **Hayden Munoz** by submission in just twenty-three seconds. She began training in jiujitsu and made her professional mixed martial arts (MMA) debut in 2011, defeating **Ediane Gomes** and kickboxing champion **Charmaine Tweet**, who both submitted in under a minute. In 2012, Rousey defeated rival Miesha Tate, earning a submission in the first round using her signature armbar and becoming the new Strikeforce Women's Bantamweight Champion. She successfully defended her title later that year against former champion **Sarah Kaufman** by submission with an armbar in 54 seconds.

A few months later, Rousey made history as the first female fighter to sign with the Ultimate Fighting Championship (UFC). UFC president Dana White had claimed for years that female fighters would never be allowed in the iconic octagon. Nevertheless, in November 2012, White announced that Rousey was the first UFC Women's Bantamweight Champion. Rousey went on to successfully defend the title six times, with an average time of 2 minutes and 59 seconds, more than five minutes faster than the average time of a single match in every UFC weight class.

In November 2015, Rousey's record-setting reign as champion ended when she was defeated by kickboxer **Holly Holm**—her first ever UFC loss. A year later, Rousey was defeated once again by Brazilian fighter **Amanda Nunes**, whose quick punches ended the match with a technical knockout after only 48 seconds. Rousey's MMA career came to a close, and she became the first female fighter inducted into the UFC Hall of Fame in 2018.

Rousey, a professional wrestling fan, announced in January 2018 that she was joining World Wrestling Entertainment (WWE) and won the Raw Women's Championship that August, becoming the first woman to win a championship in both the UFC and WWE.

Regarded as one of the greatest soccer players in history, forward **LIONEL MESSI** helped his club take more than two dozen league titles and tournaments and led the Argentina senior national team to win their first major tournament in nearly two decades.

Born in 1987 in Rosario, Argentina, Messi began playing soccer as a young child. He was small for his age due to a hormone deficiency, but he quickly showed promise in the sport and was recruited to join the youth soccer club in his hometown. At the age of thirteen, Messi was invited to train in the youth academy for FC Barcelona, one of the most successful club teams in Europe.

Messi made his first appearance for FC Barcelona in 2005, making history at the age of sixteen as the youngest player ever to score a goal for the team. Messi's speed, agility, and relentless attacks combined with his short stature prompted many to compare Messi to Argentinian great **Diego Maradona** (see no. 74), and Messi soon proved these speculations to be true. He led Barcelona to major successes, and in 2009, notably won the Champions League, La Liga, and Spanish Super Cup titles. That year he won his first Ballon d'Or Award and the FIFA World Player of the Year Award, both by the greatest voting margin in history.

Even though he was already at the top of the soccer world, Messi continued to improve. He won the Champions League title again in 2011 and continued to set astonishing records. In 2012, he became the first player to score five goals in a Champions League match, and just a few weeks later, became Barcelona's all-time goal scorer, surpassing **Cesar Rodriguez's** record of 232 goals. By the end of the year, Messi broken the record for goals scored in a single year. Then, a few months later, he became the first player in history to win a fourth Ballon d'Or award—only to win it again for the fifth time in 2015. He was named captain in 2018, and won a record-breaking sixth Ballon d'Or in 2019, breaking his tie with Portuguese star **Cristiano Ronaldo**. In August 2021, Messi surprised the soccer world by leaving FC Barcelona after nearly eighteen years for Paris St. Germain FC.

Despite Messi's club success, he seemed simply unable to lead the Argentina national team to any major victories. Though Messi was named player of the tournament in the 2014 World Cup, Argentina lost in the final to Germany. They suffered disappointment at the 2015 and 2016 Copa America tournaments when they were beaten in the final by Chile both times. They were hopeful as they went into the 2018 World Cup, but again failed to win the title after losing to France in the round of sixteen. Finally, at the 2021 Copa America tournament and in his 151st appearance for his country, Messi enjoyed his first major win for Argentina when they defeated host Brazil in the final 1–0.

With over 750 career goals, countless records and international awards, and unmatched skill, Messi firmly established himself as an undisputable great of his sport.

Professional football quarterback turned civil rights activist **COLIN KAEPERNICK** not only made a name for himself during his six seasons with the San Francisco 49ers but became an icon and subject of controversy due to his highly publicized peaceful protest against police brutality and racial injustice.

Kaepernick was born in 1987 in Milwaukee, Wisconsin, and was adopted by his parents when he was five weeks old. His family moved to California when he was four years old, and when he was eight, he began playing youth football. Kaepernick played multiple sports in high school, and even received several scholarship offers to play collegiate baseball, but in 2006, he signed to play football for The University of Nevada, Reno.

At the end of his sophomore season at Nevada, Kaepernick was named the Western Athletic Conference (WAC) Offensive Player of the Year. In November 2010, Kaepernick led his team to victory over the Boise State Broncos, ending their twenty-four-game win streak. Kaepernick graduated with a 4.0 GPA and bachelor's degree in business management. In 2011, he was drafted to the 49ers in the second round at the NFL draft.

Kaepernick scored his first professional touchdown in 2012 and took over as the team's top quarterback. In his first postseason start, Kaepernick set a new NFL single game record for a quarterback after rushing 181 yards against the Green Bay Packers. The 49ers won the National Football Conference (NFC) Championship game but went on to lose Super Bowl XLVII to the Baltimore Ravens. But by 2015, Kaepernick was replaced as starting quarterback and suffered a shoulder injury that kept him off the field.

During the first few 2016 preseason games, Kaepernick chose to remain seated during the national anthem to protest police brutality against Black Americans, including the fatal shootings of Alton Sterling and Philando Castile. His seated protest went largely unnoticed, though after speaking with former NFL player and U.S. military veteran Nate Boyer, Kaepernick began to kneel on the field during the anthem to continue his goal of peacefully protesting while still displaying respect for members of the military and veterans. This protest was more visible and sparked major controversy. Some observers praised Kaepernick's patriotism and effort to bring awareness to social issues. Others resented what they viewed as bringing politics into sports and called Kaepernick's actions disrespectful. Kaepernick continued kneeling for the entire 2016–2017 season. In September 2017, criticism intensified when then-President Donald Trump called for the NFL to fire players who chose to kneel, even though the NFL had no rules that barred this action. In response to these remarks, over 200 NFL players knelt in protest on September 24, 2017.

Kaepernick became a free agent in 2017 and found himself without any contract offers. In October 2017, Kaepernick filed a grievance against the NFL, alleging that league owners were keeping him from playing due to his political statements. In 2019, he reached a confidential settlement with the NFL and withdrew the grievance but remained unsigned.

Taking a knee has become a more common and iconic form of protest, now utilized by athletes at all levels all over the world.

One of the most inspiring athletes of her time, **BETHANY HAMILTON**'s determination and passion for her sport in the face of adversity has secured her place in sports history.

Hamilton was born on Kaua'i, Hawaii, in 1990, to a surfing family. Alongside her two older brothers, she learned to surf at the age of three. Hamilton began competitive surfing by eight, and showing great talent in the sport,

earned her first sponsorship the following year. Soon, she was winning competitions, beating out older and more competitive surfers. By thirteen, she won second place in the open women's division of the National Scholastic Surfing Association (NSSA) National Championships in San Clemente, California.

On October 31, 2003, Hamilton set out with her best friend, Alana Blanchard, to surf at Tunnels Beach in Hā'ena. Hamilton was lying on her board when her left arm, which had been dangling in the water, was suddenly pulled intensely by something underwater, and she was pulled back and forth on her board. When the incident was over a few moments later, Hamilton noticed that the water around her had turned red, and Blanchard saw that her friend's arm had been severed. Hamilton found out later that she had been attacked by a fourteen-foot tiger shark. Blanchard's father, who was with the girls, fashioned a tourniquet for Hamilton's arm from his surfboard leash and rushed her to the hospital. She lost over sixty percent of her blood by the time she arrived at the hospital and was in shock. After

several surgeries, she was released from the hospital in a few days.

Despite the trauma and major injury, thirteen-year-old Hamilton was determined to overcome these obstacles and continue surfing. Only twenty-six days after the shark attack, Hamilton courageously got back on her board. To make it easier to paddle with only one arm, Hamilton initially used a custom-made surfboard that was slightly longer and thicker than a standard one, and had a handle for her right arm. She also taught herself to kick more to make up for the loss of her left arm.

Hamilton was intent on fulfilling her surfing goals, and to the amazement of many, soon returned to competition. After the accident, she won fifth place in at her first major competition in January 2004. She continued training, and earned first place in several competitions, including the 18-and-under division of the NSSA National Championship in 2004 and 2005.

Hamilton was awarded an ESPY Award for Best Comeback Athlete in 2004, and that same year released her book *Soul Surfer* about her attack and determination to continue surfing against all odds. She continued surfing professionally, competing internationally in World Surf League events, and has become one of the most noted and leading professional surfers of all time. In 2016, a year after giving birth to her first child, she placed third in the Fiji Women's Pro competition, beating out six-time world champion Stephanie Gilmore. She was inducted into the Surfer's Hall of Fame in 2017.

TRIVIA QUESTIONS

TEST YOUR knowledge and challenge your friends with the following questions. The answers are contained in the biographies noted.

1. Which sport is a famous Roman emperor credited with establishing as a pastime? (See no. 4)

2. Who overcame a childhood disease that left him confined to a wheelchair and later became an Olympic champion? (See no. 9)

3. Why did a "long count" in a boxing match cost a fighter his chance to regain the heavyweight championship of the world? (See no. 15)

4. How did a legendary college running back help professional football gain widespread acceptance with the public? (See no. 19)

5. How did one longtime Montreal Canadiens goalie significantly influence the sport of hockey? (See no. 33)

6. Where did one of pro basketball's greatest centers first get national recognition as an outstanding collegiate player? (See no. 40)

7. Who is the only tennis player to have twice won all four Grand Slam tournaments in one year? (See no. 45)

8. How did a skier who never had a skiing lesson in her life win six World Cup titles during the 1970s? (See no. 62)

9. When did a championship tennis star become the oldest person ever to win a Grand Slam event? (See no. 70)

10. Which speed skater holds more Olympic medals than any other American female athlete? (See no. 83)

11. Who overcame a life-threatening illness to become a world champion cyclist? (See no. 85)

12. Who became the first African American woman to be named prima ballerina of the American Ballet Theatre? (See no. 91)

13. Who was the first American woman to win an Olympic medal in judo? (See no. 97)

14. What athlete is known for beginning the practice of athletes kneeling during the national anthem as a form of protest? (See no. 99)

PROJECT SUGGESTIONS

1. Choose one of the athletes from this book and write a one-page fictional diary entry for one day in that person's life. Pick a day that had some significance for the individual. For example, you could write about the day he or she had a great performance in an athletic event or achieved some other noteworthy success. Or choose a day on which the person had a personal setback or was frustrated in some way by their lack of success. Describe the person's thoughts and feelings in as much detail as you can.

2. Arrange a "meeting" of two of the people in this book who could never have met in real life. You can choose two athletes from the same sport who never competed against each other or two from different fields of athletic competition, but they must be from different eras (for example, Sonja Henie and Michelle Kwan, or Phidippides and Lionel Messi). Imagine what their meeting would be like. Write one to two pages describing the scenario and create dialogue between the two people. What kinds of questions do you think they would ask each other? Would they approve of the things that each had done in their lifetimes? Be as imaginative as you can.

INDEX

OUT NOW: